Archibald H. Sayce

Fresh Light from the Ancient Monuments

a sketch of the most striking confirmations of the Bible, from recent discoveries in

Egypt, Palestine, Assyria, Babylonia, Asia Minor. Second Edition

Archibald H. Sayce

Fresh Light from the Ancient Monuments
a sketch of the most striking confirmations of the Bible, from recent discoveries in Egypt,
Palestine, Assyria, Babylonia, Asia Minor. Second Edition

ISBN/EAN: 9783337248031

Printed in Europe, USA, Canada, Australia, Japan

Cover: Foto ©Andreas Hilbeck / pixelio.de

More available books at **www.hansebooks.com**

Monument of a Hittite king, accompanied by an inscription in Hittite hieroglyphics, discovered on the site of Carchemish and now in the British Museum.

By-Paths of Bible Knowledge.

III.

FRESH LIGHT FROM THE ANCIENT MONUMENTS.

A SKETCH OF THE MOST STRIKING CONFIRMATIONS OF THE
BIBLE, FROM RECENT DISCOVERIES IN

EGYPT.   PALESTINE.

ASSYRIA.   BABYLONIA.

ASIA MINOR.

BY

A. H. SAYCE, M.A.

Deputy Professor of Comparative Philology, Oxford,
Hon. LL.D., Dublin.

SECOND EDITION.

THE RELIGIOUS TRACT SOCIETY:

56, PATERNOSTER ROW; 65, ST. PAUL'S CHURCHYARD.

1884.

PREFACE.

———◆———

THE object of this little book is explained by its title. Discovery after discovery has been pouring in upon us from Oriental lands, and the accounts given only ten years ago of the results of Oriental research are already beginning to be antiquated. It is useful, therefore, to take stock of our present knowledge, and to see how far it bears out that "old story" which has been familiar to us from our childhood. The same spirit of scepticism which had rejected the early legends of Greece and Rome had laid its hands also on the Old Testament, and had determined that the sacred histories themselves were but a collection of myths and fables. But suddenly, as with the wand of a magician, the ancient eastern world has been reawakened to life by the spade of the explorer and the patient skill of the decipherer, and we now find ourselves in the presence of monuments which bear the names or recount the deeds of the heroes of Scripture. One by one these "stones crying out" have been examined or more perfectly explained, while others of equal importance are being continually added to them.

A

What striking confirmations of the Bible narrative have been afforded by the latest discoveries will be seen from the following pages. In many cases confirmation has been accompanied by illustration. Unexpected light has been thrown upon facts and statements hitherto obscure, or a wholly new explanation has been given of some event recorded by the inspired writer. What can be more startling than the discovery of the great Hittite Empire, the very existence of which had been forgotten, and which yet once contended on equal terms with Egypt on the one side and Assyria on the other? The allusions to the Hittites in the Old Testament, which had been doubted by a sceptical criticism, have been shown to be fully in accordance with the facts, and their true place in history has been pointed out.

But the account of the Hittite Empire is not the only discovery of the last four or five years about which this book has to speak. Inscriptions of Sargon have cleared up the difficulties attending the tenth and eleventh chapters of Isaiah's prophecies, and have proved that no "ideal" campaign of an "ideal" Assyrian king is described in them. The campaign, on the contrary, was a very real one, and when Isaiah delivered his prophecy the Assyrian monarch was marching down upon Jerusalem from the north, and was about to be "the rod" of God's anger upon its sins. Ten years before the overthrow of Sennacherib's army his father, Sargon, had captured Jerusalem, but a "remnant" escaped the horrors of the siege, and returned in penitence "unto the mighty God."

Perhaps the most remarkable of recent discoveries is that which relates to Cyrus and his conquest of Babylonia. The history of the conquest as told by Cyrus himself is now in our hands, and it has obliged us to modify many of the views, really derived from Greek authors, which we had read into the words of Scripture. Cyrus, we know now upon his own authority, was a polytheist, and not a Zoroastrian; he was king of Elam, not of Persia. It was Elam, and not Persia, as Isaiah's prophecies declared, which invaded Babylon. Babylon itself was taken without a siege, and Mr. Bosanquet may therefore have been right in holding that the Darius of Daniel was Darius the son of Hystaspes.

Hardly less interesting has been the discovery of the inscription of Siloam, which reveals to us the very characters used by the Jews in the time of Isaiah, perhaps even in the time of Solomon himself. The discovery has cast a flood of light on the early topography of Jerusalem, and has made it clear as the daylight that the Jews of the royal period were not the rude and barbarous people it has been the fashion of an unbelieving criticism to assume, but a cultured and literary population. Books must have been as plentiful among them as they were in Phœnicia or Assyria; nor

must we forget the results of the excavations undertaken last year in the land of Goshen. Pithom, the
treasure-city built by the Israelites, has been disinterred,
and the date of the Exodus has been fixed. M. Naville
has even found there bricks made without straw.

But the old records of Egypt and Assyria have a
further interest than a merely historical one. They tell
us what were the religious doctrines and aspirations of
those who composed them, and what was their conception of their duty towards God and man. We have only
to compare the hymns and psalms and prayers of these
ancient peoples—seeking "the Lord, if haply they might
feel after Him and find Him"—with the fuller lights
revealed in the pages of the Old Testament, to discover
how wide was the chasm that lay between the two.
The one was seeking what the other had already found.
The Hebrew prophet was the forerunner and herald of
the Gospel, and the light shed by the Gospel had been
reflected back upon him. He saw already "the Sun of
Righteousness" rising in the east; the psalmist of
Shinar or the devout worshipper of Asshur were like
unto those "upon whom no day has dawned."

CONTENTS.

CHAPTER IV.

THE MOABITE STONE AND THE INSCRIPTION OF SILOAM.

CHAPTER V.

THE EMPIRE OF THE HITTITES.

CHAPTER VI.

THE ASSYRIAN INVASIONS.

CHAPTER VII.

NEBUCHADREZZAR AND CYRUS.

LIST OF ILLUSTRATIONS.

———◆———

FRESH LIGHT FROM THE ANCIENT MONUMENTS.

CHAPTER I.

INTRODUCTION.

How the Cuneiform Inscriptions were deciphered.—Grotefend's guess.— Lassen and Rawlinson's studies.—Discoveries of Botta, Layard, George Smith, and Rassam.—Certainty of our present knowledge.

THE decipherment of the cuneiform or wedge-shaped inscriptions of Assyria has been one of the most marvellous achievements of the present century. It has often been asked how Assyrian scholars have been enabled to read an Assyrian text with almost as much certainty as a page of the Old Testament, although both the language and the characters in which it is written were utterly unknown but a few years ago. A brief history of the origin and progress of the decipherment will best answer the question.

Travellers had discovered inscriptions engraved in cuneiform, or, as they were also termed, arrow-headed, characters on the ruined monuments of Persepolis and other ancient, sites in Persia. Some of these monuments were known to have been erected by the Achæmenian princes—Darius, the son of Hystaspes, and his successors —and it was therefore inferred that the inscriptions also had been carved by order of the same kings. The inscriptions were in three different systems of cuneiform writing ; and, since the three kinds of inscription were always placed side by side, it was evident that they represented different versions of the same text. The subjects of the Persian kings belonged to more than one race, and just as in the present day a Turkish pasha in the East has to publish an edict in Turkish, Arabic, and Persian, if it is to be understood by all the populations under his charge, so the Persian kings were obliged to use the language and system of writing peculiar to each of the nations they governed, whenever they wished their proclamations to be read and understood by them.

It was clear that the three versions of the Achæmenian inscriptions were addressed to the three chief populations of the Persian Empire, and that the one which invariably came first was composed in ancient Persian, the language of the sovereign himself. Now this Persian version happened to offer the decipherer less difficulties than the two others which accompanied it. The number of distinct characters employed in writing it did not exceed forty, while the words were divided from one another by a slanting wedge. Some of the words contained so many characters that it was plain that these latter must denote letters, and not syllables, and that consequently the Persian cuneiform system must have consisted of an alphabet, and not of a syllabary. It was further plain that the inscriptions had to be read from left to right, since the ends of all the lines were exactly underneath one another on the left side, whereas they terminated irregularly on the right ; indeed, the last line sometimes ended at a considerable distance from the right-hand extremity of the inscription.

The clue to the decipherment of the inscriptions was first discovered by the successful guess of a German scholar, Grotefend. Grotefend noticed that the inscriptions generally began with three or four words, one of which varied, while the others remained unchanged. The variable word had three forms, though the same form always appeared on the same monument. Grotefend, therefore, conjectured that this word represented the name of a king, the words which followed it being the royal titles. One of the supposed names appeared much oftener than the others, and as it was too short for Artaxerxes and too long for Cyrus, it was evident that it must stand either for Darius or for Xerxes. A study of the classical authors showed Grotefend that certain of the monuments on which it was found had been constructed by Darius, and he accordingly gave to the characters composing it the values required for spelling "Darius" in its old Persian form. In this way he succeeded in obtaining conjectural values for six cuneiform letters. He now turned to the second royal name, which also appeared on several monuments, and was of much the same length as that of Darius. This could only be Xerxes ; but if so, the fifth letter composing it (*r*) would necessarily be the same as the third letter in the name of Darius. This proved to be the case, and thus afforded the best possible evidence that the German scholar was on the right track.

The third name, which was much longer than the other two, differed from the second chiefly at the beginning, the latter part of it resembling the name of Xerxes. Clearly, therefore, it could be nothing else than Artaxerxes, and that it actually was so, was rendered certain by the fact that the second character composing it was that which had the value of *r*.

Grotefend now possessed a small alphabet, and with this he proceeded to read the word which always followed the royal name, and therefore probably meant "king."

He found that it closely resembled the word which signified " king " in Zend, the old language of the Eastern
Persians, which was spoken in one part of Persia at
the same time that Old Persian, the language of the
Achæmenian princes, was spoken in another. There
could, consequently, be no further room for doubt that he
had really solved the great problem, and discovered
the key to the decipherment of the cuneiform texts.

But he did little further himself towards the completion of the work, and it was many years before any real
progress was made with it. Meanwhile, the study of
Zend had made great advances, more especially in the
hands of Burnouf, who eventually turned his attention to
the cuneiform inscriptions. But it is to Burnouf's pupil,
Lassen, as well as to Sir Henry Rawlinson, that the
decipherment of these inscriptions owes its final completion. The discovery of the list of Persian satrapies in
the inscription of Darius at Naksh-i-Rustem, and above
all the copy of the long inscription of Darius on the rock
of Behistun, made by Sir H. Rawlinson, enabled these
scholars independently of one another to construct an
alphabet which differed only in the value assigned to a
single character, and, with the help of the cognate Zend
and Sanskrit, to translate the language so curiously
brought to light. The decipherment of the Persian
cuneiform texts thus became an accomplished fact ;
what was next needed was to decipher the two
versions which were inscribed at their side.

But this was no easy task. The words in them were
not divided from one another, and the characters of
which they were composed were exceedingly numerous.
With the assistance, however, of frequently recurring
proper names even these two versions gradually yielded

to the patient skill of the decipherer; and it was then discovered that while one of them represented an agglutinative language, such as that of the Turks or Fins, the other was in a dialect which closely resembled the Hebrew of the Old Testament. The monuments found almost immediately afterwards in Assyria and Babylonia by Botta and Layard soon made it clear to what people this dialect must have belonged. The inscriptions of Nineveh turned out to be written in the same language and form of cuneiform script; and it must therefore have been for the Semitic population of Assyria and Babylonia that the kings of Persia had caused one of the versions of their inscriptions to be drawn up. This version served as a starting-point for the decipherment of the texts which the excavations in Assyria had brought to light.

It might have been thought that the further course of the decipherment would have presented little difficulty, now that the values of many of the Assyrian characters were known, and the close resemblance of the language they concealed to Hebrew had been discovered. But the complicated nature of the Assyrian system of cuneiform—the great number of characters used in it, the different phonetic values the same character might have, and the frequent employment of ideographs, which denoted ideas and not sounds—caused the progress of decipherment to be for some time but slow. Indeed, had the Assyrian inscriptions been confined to those engraved on the alabaster bulls and other monuments of Nineveh, our knowledge of the language would always have remained comparatively limited. But, fortunately, the Assyrians, like the Babylonians before them, employed clay as a writing material, and established libraries, which were filled with a literature on baked bricks.

One of the most important results of Sir A. H. Layard's explorations at Nineveh was the discovery of the ruined library of the ancient city, now buried under the mounds of Kouyunjik. The broken clay tablets belonging to this library not only furnished the student with an immense mass of literary matter, but also with direct aids towards a knowledge of the Assyrian syllabary and language. Among the literature represented in the library of Kouyunjik were lists of characters, with their various phonetic and ideographic meanings, tables of synonymes, and catalogues of the names of plants and animals. This, however, was not all. The inventors of the cuneiform system of writing had been a people who preceded the Semites in the occupation of Babylonia, and who spoke an agglutinative language utterly different from that of their Semitic successors. These Accadians, as they are usually termed, left behind them a considerable amount of literature, which was highly prized by the Semitic Babylonians and Assyrians. A large portion of the Ninevite tablets, accordingly, consists of interlinear or parallel translations from Accadian into Assyrian, as well as of reading books, dictionaries, and grammars, in which the Accadian original is placed by the side of its Assyrian equivalent. It frequently happens that the signification of a previously unknown Assyrian word can be ascertained by our finding it given as the rendering of an Accadian word, with the meaning of which we are already acquainted. The bilingual texts have not only enabled scholars to recover the long-forgotten Accadian language ; they have also been of the greatest possible assistance to them in their reconstruction of the Assyrian dictionary itself.

The three expeditions conducted by Mr. George Smith, as well as the later ones of Mr. Hormuzd Rassam, have added largely to the stock of tablets from Kouyunjik originally acquired for the British Museum by Sir A. H. Layard, and have also brought to light a few other tablets from the libraries of Babylonia. Although, therefore, only one of the many libraries which now lie buried beneath the ground in Babylonia and Assyria has, as yet, been at all adequately explored, the amount of Assyrian literature at the disposal of the student is already greater than that contained in the whole of the Old Testament. Apart from the help afforded by the old dictionaries and lists of words and characters, he has more facilities for determining the meaning of a word by a comparison of parallel passages than the student of Biblical Hebrew; and in many instances, accordingly, Assyrian has made it possible to fix the signification of a Hebrew word, the sense of which has hitherto been doubtful.

The Assyrian student, moreover, possesses an advantage which is not shared by the Hebraist. Owing to its hieroglyphic origin, the cuneiform system of writing makes large use of what are called determinatives, that is to say, of characters which have no phonetic value, but which determine the class to which the word they accompany belongs. It is, therefore, always possible to tell at a glance whether the word with which we are dealing is the name of a man, of a woman, of a deity, of a river, of a country, or of a city; or, again, whether it denotes an animal, a bird, a vegetable, a stone, a star, a medicine, or the like. With all these aids, accordingly, it is not wonderful that the study of Assyrian has made immense progress during the last few years, and that an

ordinary historical text can be read with as much certainty as a page from one of the historical books of the
Old Testament. Indeed, we may say that it can be read
with even greater certainty, since it presents us with the
actual words of the original writer ; whereas the text of
the Old Testament has come to us through the hands of
successive generations of copyists, who have corrupted
many passages so as to make them grammatically un-
intelligible.

At the same time, the hieroglyphic origin of the
cuneiform mode of writing has been productive of dis-
advantages as well as of advantages. The characters
which compose it may express ideas as well as sounds ;
and though we may know what ideas are represented,
we may not always know the exact pronunciation to be
assigned to them. Thus, in English, the ideograph +
may be pronounced "plus," "added to," or "more,"
according to the pleasure of the reader. The Assyrian
scribes usually attached one or more phonetic characters
to the ideographs they employed, in order to indicate
their pronunciation in a given passage ; but these "phonetic complements," as they are termed, were frequently
omitted in the case of well-known proper names, such as
those of the native kings and deities. Hence the exact
pronunciation of these names can only be settled when
we find them written phonetically ; and there are one
or two proper names, such as that of the hero of the
great Chaldean epic, which have never yet been met
with phonetically spelt.

Another disadvantage due to the hieroglyphic origin
of the Assyrian syllabary is the number of different phonetic values the same character may bear. This caused
a good deal of trouble in the early days of Assyrian

decipherment ; but it was a difficulty that was felt quite
as much by the Assyrians themselves as it is by us.
Consequently they adopted various devices for over-
coming it ; and as these devices have become known the
difficulty has ceased to be felt.   In short, the study of
Assyrian now reposes on as sure and certain a basis as
the study of any ancient language, a knowledge of which
has been traditionally handed down to us ; and the
antiquity of its monuments, the copiousness of its voca-
bulary, the perfection of its grammar, and the syllabic
character of the writing—which expresses vowels as well
as consonants—all combine to make it of the highest
importance for the study of the Semitic languages.
Its recovery has not only shed a flood of light on the
history and antiquities of the Old Testament, it has
served to illustrate and explain the language of the Old
Testament as well.

CHAPTER II.

THE BOOK OF GENESIS.

Recent discoveries, especially in Babylonia and Assyria, have thrown much light on Genesis.—The Accadians.—An Assyrian account of the Creation.—The Babylonian Sabbath.—Traces of an account of the Fall. —Site of Paradise.—" Adam" a Babylonian word.—The Chaldean story of the Deluge.—This compared with the record in Genesis.—The Babylonian account of the building of Babel.—The light thrown by the Assyrian inscriptions on the names in Gen. x.—Gomer; Madai; Javan; Cush and Mizraim; Phut; Canaan; Elam; Asshur; Arphaxad; Aram; Lud; Nimrod.—The site of Ur.—Approximate date of the rescue of Lot by Abraham.—Egypt in the time of Abraham.—Records of famines.—The date of Joseph's appointment as second ruler in Egypt.— The Tale of the Two Brothers.—Goshen.

THERE is no book in the world about which more has been written than the Bible, and perhaps there is no portion of the Bible which has given rise to a larger literature than the Book of Genesis. Every word in it has been carefully scrutinised, now by scholars who sought to discover its deepest meaning or to defend it against the attacks of adversaries, now again by hostile critics anxious to expose every supposed flaw, and to convict it of error and inconsistency. Assailants and defenders had long to content themselves with such evidence as could be derived from a study of the book itself, or from the doubtful traditions of ancient nations, as reported by the writers of Greece and Rome. Such reports were alike imperfect and untrustworthy ; historical criticism was still in its infancy in the age of the classical authors, and they cared but little to describe

accurately the traditions of races whom they despised.
It was even a question whether any credit could be
given to the fragments of Egyptian, Babylonian, and
Phœnician mythology or history extracted by Christian
apologists from the lost works of native authors who
wrote in Greek. The Egyptian dynasties of Manetho,
the Babylonian stories of the Creation and Flood narrated by Berossus, the self-contradicting Phœnician
legends collected by Philo Byblius, were all more or
less suspected of being an invention of a later age.
The earlier chapters of Genesis stood almost alone ;
friends and foes alike felt the danger of resting any
argument on the apparent similarity of the accounts
recorded in them to the myths and legends contained
in the fragments of Manetho, of Berossus, and of Philo
Byblius.

All is changed now. The marvellous discoveries of
the last half-century have thrown a flood of light on the
ancient oriental world, and some of this light has necessarily been reflected on the Book of Genesis. The
monuments of Egypt, of Babylonia, and of Assyria have
been rescued from their hiding-places, and the writing
upon them has been made to speak once more in living
words. A dead world has been called again to life by
the spade of the excavator and the patient labour of the
decipherer. We find ourselves, as it were, face to face
with Sennacherib, with Nebuchadnezzar, and with
Cyrus, with those whose names have been familiar to us
from childhood, but who have hitherto been to us mere
names, mere shadowy occupants of an unreal world.
Thanks to the research of the last half-century, we can
now penetrate into the details of their daily life, can
examine their religious ideas, can listen to them as they

themselves recount the events of their own time or the traditions of the past which had been handed down to them.

It is more especially in Babylonia and Assyria that we find illustrations of the earlier chapters of Genesis, as, indeed, is only natural. The Semitic language spoken in these two countries was closely allied to that of the Old Testament, as closely, in fact, as two modern English dialects are allied to each other; and it was from Babylonia, from Ur of the Chaldees, now represented by the mounds of Mugheir, that Abraham made his way to the future home of his descendants in the west. It is to Babylonia that the Biblical accounts of the Fall, of the Deluge, and of the Confusion of Tongues particularly look: two of the rivers of Paradise were the Tigris and Euphrates, the ark rested on the mountains of Ararat, and the city built around the Tower which men designed should reach to heaven was Babel or Babylon. Babylonia was an older kingdom than Assyria, which took its name from the city of Assur, now Kalah Sherghat, on the Tigris, the original capital of the country. It was divided into two halves, Accad (Gen. x. 10) being Northern Babylonia, and Sumir, the Shinar of the Old Testament, Southern Babylonia. The primitive populations of both Sumir and Accad were related, not to the Semitic race, but to the tribes which continued to maintain themselves in the mountains of Elam down to a late day. They spoke two cognate dialects, which were agglutinative in character, like the languages of the modern Turks and Fins; that is to say, the relations of grammar were expressed by coupling words together, each of which retained an independent meaning of its own. Thus *in-nin-sun* is "he gave it," literally "he-it-gave," *e-mes-na* is "of houses," literally "house-many-of." At an early date, which cannot yet, however, be exactly determined, the Sumirians and Accadians were overrun and conquered by the Semitic Babylonians of later history, Accad being apparently the first half of the country to fall under the sway of the new-comers. It is possible that Casdim, the Hebrew word translated "Chaldees" or "Chaldæans" in the Authorised Version, is the Babylonian *casidi*, or "conquerors," a title which continued to cling to them in consequence of their conquest.

The Accadians had been the inventors of the pictorial hieroglyphics which afterwards developed into the cuneiform or wedge-shaped system of writing; they had founded the great cities of Chaldea, and had attained to a high degree of culture and civilisation. Their cities possessed libraries, stocked with books, written partly on papyrus, partly on clay, which was, while still soft, impressed with characters by means of a metal stylus. The books were numerous, and related to a variety of subjects. Among them there were more particularly two to which a special degree of sanctity was attached. One of these contained magical formulæ for warding off the assaults of evil spirits; the other was a collection of hymns to the gods, which was used by the priests as a kind of prayer-book. When the Semitic Babylonians, the kinsmen of the Hebrews, the Aramæans, the Phœnicians and the Arabs, conquered the old population, they received from it, along with other elements of culture, the cuneiform system of writing and the literature written in it. The sacred hymns still continued to serve as a prayer-book, but they were now provided with interlinear translations into the Babylonian (or, as it is usually termed, the Assyrian) language. Part of the literature consisted of legal codes and decisions ; and since the inheritance and holding of property frequently depended on a knowledge of these, it became necessary for the conquerors to acquaint themselves with the language of the people they had conquered. In course of time, however, the two dialects of Sumir and Accad ceased to be spoken ; but the necessity for learning them still remained, and we find accordingly that down to the latest days of both Assyria and Babylonia the educated classes were taught the old extinct Accadian, just as in modern Europe they are taught Latin. From time to time, indeed, the scribes of Sennacherib or Nebuchadnezzar attempted to write in the ancient language, and in doing so some-times made similar mistakes to those that are made now-a-days by a schoolboy in writing Latin.

The Accadians were, like the Chinese, pre-eminently a literary people. Their conception of chaos was that of a period when as yet no books were written. Ac-cordingly, a legend of the Creation, preserved in the library of Cuthah, contains this curious statement : " On a memorial-tablet none wrote, none explained, for bodies and produce were not brought forth in the earth." To the author of the legend the art of writing seemed to mount back to the very beginning of man-kind.

This legend of the Creation, however, is not the only one that has been recovered from the shipwreck of Assyrian and Babylonian literature. Besides the account given in the fragments of Berossus, there is another, which bears a striking resemblance to the account of the Creation in the first chapter of Genesis.

It does not appear, however, that this last was of Accadian origin ; at all events, there is no indication that it was translated into Assyrian from an older Accadian document, and there are even reasons for thinking that it may not be earlier—in its present form at least—than the seventh century B.C. We possess, unfortunately, only portions of it, since many of the series of clay tablets on which it was inscribed have been lost or injured.   The account begins as follows :—

1. At that time the heavens above named not a name,
2. Nor did the earth below record one :
3. Yea, the deep was their first creator,
4. The flood of the sea was she who bore them all.
5. Their waters were embosomed in one place, and
6. The flowering reed was ungathered, the marsh-plant was ungrown.
7. At that time the gods had not issued forth, any one of them,
8. By no name were they recorded, no destiny (had they fixed).
9. Then the (great) gods were made,
10. Lakhmu and Lakhamu issued forth (the first),
11. They grew up . . . . .
12. Next were made the host of heaven and earth,
13. The time was long (and then)
14. The gods Anu (Bel and Ea were born of)
15. The host of heaven and earth.

It is not until we come to the fifth tablet of the series, which describes the appointment of the heavenly bodies —the work of the fourth day of creation, according to Genesis—that the narrative is again preserved.   Here we read that the Creator " made beautiful the stations of the great gods," or stars, an expression which reminds us of the oft-recurring phrase of Genesis : " And God saw that it was good." The stars, moon, and sun were ordered to rule over the night and day, and to determine the year, with its months and days. The latter part of the tablet, however, like the latter part of the first tablet, is destroyed, and of the next tablet—that which described the creation of animals—only the first few lines remain. "At that time," it begins, "the gods in their assembly created (the living creatures). They made beautiful the mighty (animals). They made the living beings come forth, the cattle of the field, the beast of the field, and the creeping thing." What follows is too mutilated to yield a connected sense.

There is no need of pointing out how closely this Assyrian account of the Creation resembles that of Genesis. Even the very wording and phrases of Genesis occur in it, and though no fragment is preserved which expressly tells us that the work of the Creation was accomplished in seven days, we may infer that such was the case, from the order of events as recorded on the tablets. But, with all this similarity, there is even greater dissimilarity. The philosophical conceptions with which the Assyrian account opens, the polytheistic colouring which we find in it further on, have no parallel in the Book of Genesis. The spirit of the two narratives is essentially different.

The last tablet probably contained an account of the institution of the Sabbath. At all events, we learn that the seventh day was observed as a day of rest among the Babylonians, as it was among the Jews. It was even called by the same name of Sabbath, a word which is defined in an Assyrian text as "a day of rest for the heart," while the Accadian equivalent is explained to mean "a day of completion of labour." A calendar of saints' days for the month of the intercalary Elul makes the seventh, fourteenth, twenty-first, and twenty-eighth days of the lunar month Sabbaths, on which certain works were forbidden to be done. On those days, it is stated, " flesh cooked on the fire may not be eaten, the clothing of the body may not be changed, white garments may not be put on, a sacrifice may not be offered, the king may not ride in his chariot, nor speak in public, the augur may not mutter in a secret place, medicine of the body may not be applied, nor may any curse be uttered." Nothing, in fact, that implied work was allowed to be done. Where the Babylonian Sabbath differed from the Jewish one was in its essentially lunar character. The first Sabbath was the first day of a month, whatever might be the length of the month that preceded it. While Sabbaths and new moons are distinguished from one another in the Old Testament, they are found united in the Babylonian ritual. It is no wonder, therefore, that the Babylonians were acquainted with a week of seven days, each day of which was dedicated to one of the seven planets ; it was the space of time naturally marked out by the four quarters of the moon.

No account of the Fall of Man, similar to that in Genesis, has as yet been found among the fragments of the Assyrian libraries. Mr. George Smith, indeed, supposed that he had discovered one, but the text which he referred to the Fall, is really an ancient hymn to the Creator. It is, nevertheless, pretty certain that such an account once existed. An archaic Babylonian gem represents a tree, on either side of which are seated a man and woman, with a serpent behind them, and their hands are stretched out towards the

fruit that hangs from the tree.   A few stray references in
the bilingual (Accadian and Assyrian) dictionaries throw
some light upon this representation, and inform us that
the Accadians knew of "a wicked serpent," "the
serpent of night" and "darkness," which had brought
about the fall of man.   The tree of life, of which so
many illustrations occur on Assyrian monuments, is
declared to be "the pine-tree" of Eridu, "the shrine of
the god Irnin;" and Irnin is a name of the Euphrates,
when regarded as the "snake-river," which encircled
the world like a rope, and was the stream of Hea, "the
snake-god of the tree of life."   The Euphrates, we must
remember, was one of the rivers of Paradise.

The site of Paradise is to be sought for in Babylonia.   The garden which God planted was in Eden,
and Eden, as we learn from the cuneiform records, was
the ancient name of the "field" or plain of Babylonia,
where the first living creatures had been created.   The
city of Eridu, which the people of Sumir called "the
good" or "holy," was, as we have seen, the shrine of
Irnin, and in the midst of a forest or garden that
once lay near it grew "the holy pine-tree," "the tree
of life."   The rivers of Eden can be found in the rivers
and canals of Babylonia.   Two of them were the
Euphrates and Tigris, called by the Accadians *id Idikla*,
"the river of Idikla," the Biblical Hiddekhel, while
Pishon is a Babylonian word signifying "canal," and
Gihon may be the Accadian Gukhan, the stream on
which Babylon stood.   Even the word *cherub* is itself
of Babylonian derivation.   It is the name given to one
of those winged monsters, with the body of a bull and
the head of a man, which are sometimes placed in the
Assyrian sculptures on either side of the tree of life.

They stood at the entrance of a Babylonian palace, and were supposed to prevent the evil spirits from entering within. The word comes from a root which means "to approach" or "be near," and perhaps originally signified one who was near to God.

Like *cherub*, *Adam* also was a Babylonian word. It has the general sense of "man," and is used in this sense both in Hebrew and in Assyrian. But as in Hebrew it has come to be the proper name of the first man, so, too, in the old Babylonian legends, the "Adamites" were "the white race" of Semitic descent, who stood in marked contrast to "the black heads" or Accadians of primitive Babylonia. Originally, however, it was this dark race itself that claimed to have been "the men" whom the god Merodach created; and it was not until after the Semitic conquest of Chaldea that the children of Adamu or Adam were supposed to denote the white Semitic population. Hence it is that the dark race continued to the last to be called the Adamatu or "red-skins," which a popular etymology connected with *Adamu* "man." Sir H. Rawlinson has suggested a parallel between the dark and white races of Babylonia and the "sons of God" and "daughters of men" of Genesis. Adam, we are told, was "the son of God" (Luke iii. 38). But nothing similar to what we read in the sixth chapter of Genesis has as yet been met with among the cuneiform records, and though these speak of giant heroes, like Ner and Etanna, who lived before the Flood, we know nothing as yet as to their parentage.

The Babylonians, however, were well aware that the Deluge had been caused by the wickedness of the human race. It has often been remarked that though traditions of a universal or a partial deluge are found all over the world, it is only in the Old Testament that the cause assigned for it is a moral one. The Chaldean account of the Deluge, discovered by Mr. George Smith, offers an exception to this rule. Here, as in Genesis, Sisuthros, the Accadian Noah, is saved from destruction on account of his piety, the rest of mankind being drowned as a punishment for their sins.

The story of the Deluge formed the subject of more than one poem among the Accadians. Two of these were amalgamated together by the author of a great epic in twelve books, which described the adventures of a solar hero whose name cannot be read with certainty, but may provisionally be pronounced Gisdhubar. The amalgamated account was introduced as an episode into the eleventh book, the whole epic being arranged upon an astronomical principle, so that each book should correspond to one of the signs of the Zodiac, the eleventh book consequently answering to Aquarius. Sisuthros, who had been translated without dying, like the Biblical Enoch, is made to tell the story himself to Gisdhubar. Gisdhubar had travelled in search of health to the shores of the river of death at the mouth of the Euphrates, and here afar off in the other world he sees and talks with Sisuthros. Fragments of several editions of the poem have been found, not only among the ruins of Nineveh, but also in Babylonia; and by fitting these together it has been possible to recover almost the whole of the original text. The translations of it made by different scholars have necessarily improved with the progress of Assyrian research, and though the first translation given to the world by Mr. George Smith was substantially correct, there were

many minor inaccuracies in it which have since had to
be corrected. The latest and best version is that which
has been published by Professor Haupt. The following
translation of the account is based upon it :—

(Col. I) " Sisuthros speaks to him, even to Gisdhubar :
Let me reveal unto thee, Gisdhubar, the story of my preservation, and the oracle of the gods let me tell to thee.
The city of Surippak, the city which, as thou knowest, is
built on the Euphrates, this city was already ancient
when the gods within it set their hearts to bring on a
deluge, even the great gods as many as there are—their
father Anu, their king the warrior Bel, their throne-
bearer Adar, their prince En-nugi. Ea, the lord of
wisdom, sat along with them, and repeated their decree :
' For their boat ! as a boat, as a boat, a hull, a hull !
hearken to their boat, and understand the hull, O man
of Surippak, son of Ubara-Tutu ; dig up the house,
build the ship, save what thou canst of the germ of life.
(The gods) will destroy the seed of life, but do thou live,
and bid the seed of life of every kind mount into the
midst of the ship. The ship which thou shalt build,
. . . cubits shall be its length in measure, . . .
cubits the content of its breadth and its height. (Above)
the deep cover it in.' I understood and spake to Ea,
my lord : ' The building of the ship which thou hast
commanded thus, if it be done by me, the children of
the people and the old men (alike will laugh at me).'
Ea opened his mouth and said, he speaks to me his
servant : '(If they laugh at thee) thou shalt say unto
them, (Every one) who has turned against me and (dis-
believes the oracle that) has been given me, . . . I
will judge above and below. (But as for thee) shut (not)
the door (until) the time comes of which I will send thee

word. (Then) enter the door of the ship, and bring into
the midst of it thy corn, thy property, and thy goods,
thy (family), thy household, thy concubines, and the
sons of the people. The cattle of the field, the wild
beasts of the field, as many as I would preserve, I will
send unto thee, and they shall keep thy door.' Sisuthros
opened his mouth and speaks; he says to Ea, his lord:
'(O my lord) no one yet has built a ship (in this fashion)
on land to contain the beasts (of the field). (The plan?)
let me see and the ship (I will build). On the land the
ship (I will build) as thou hast commanded me.' . . .

(Col. II) . . . On the fifth day (after it was begun)
in its circuit (?) fourteen measures its hull (measured);
fourteen measures measured (the roof) above it. I made
it a dwelling-house (?) . . . I enclosed it. I compacted
it six times, I divided (its passages) seven times, I
divided its interior (seven) times. Leaks for the waters
in the midst of it I cut off. I saw the rents, and what
was wanting I added. Three *sari* of bitumen I poured
over the outside. Three *sari* of bitumen I poured over
the inside. Three *sari* of men, carrying baskets, who
carried on their heads food, I provided, even a *saros* of
food for the people to eat, while two *sari* of food the
boatmen shared. To (the gods) I caused oxen to be
sacrificed; I (established offerings) each day. In (the
ship) beer, food, and wine (I collected) like the waters of
a river, and (I heaped them up) like the dust (?) of the
earth, and (in the ship) the food with my hand I placed.
(With the help) of Samas [the Sun-God] the compact-
ing of the ship was finished; (all parts of the ship) were
made strong, and I caused the tackling to be carried
above and below. (Then of my household) went two-
thirds: all that I had I heaped together; all that I had

of silver I heaped together; all that I had of gold I
heaped together; all that I had of the seed of life I
heaped together. I brought the whole up into the ship;
all my slaves and concubines, the cattle of the field, the
beasts of the field, the sons of the people, all of them,
did I bring up. The season Samas fixed, and he spake,
saying: 'In the night will I cause the heaven to rain
destruction. Enter into the midst of the ship and close
thy door.' The season came round; he spake, saying:
'In the night will I cause the heaven to rain destruction.'
Of that day I reached the evening, the day which I
watched for with fear. I entered into the midst of the
ship and shut the door, that I might close the ship. To
Buzur-sadi-rabi, the boatman, I gave the palace, with all
its goods. Then arose Mu-seri-ina-namari (The Water
of Dawn at Daylight) from the horizon of heaven (like)
a black cloud. Rimmon in the midst of it thundered, and
Nebo and the Wind-God go in front: the throne-bearers
go over mountain and plain: Nergal the mighty removes
the wicked; Adar goes overthrowing all before him.
The spirits of earth carried the flood; in their terribleness
they sweep through the land; the deluge of Rimmon
reaches unto heaven; all that was light to (darkness)
was turned.

(Col. III) (The surface) of the land like (fire?)
they wasted; (they destroyed all) life from the face
of the land; to battle against men they brought (the
waters). Brother saw not his brother; men knew not
one another. In heaven the gods feared the flood,
and sought a refuge; they ascended to the heaven of
Anu. The gods, like a dog in his kennel, crouched down
in a heap. Istar cries like a mother, the great goddess
utters her speech: 'All to clay is turned, and the evil I

prophesied in the presence of the gods, according as I
prophesied evil in the presence of the gods, for the
destruction of my people I prophesied (it) against them ;
and though I their mother have begotten my people, like
the spawn of the fishes they fill the sea.' Then the gods
were weeping with her because of the spirits of earth ;
the gods on a throne were seated in weeping ; covered
were their lips because of the coming evil. Six days
and nights the wind, the flood, and the storm go on
overwhelming. The seventh day when it approached
the storm subsided, the flood which had fought against
(men) like an armed host was quieted. The sea began
to dry, and the wind and the flood ended. I watched
the sea making a noise, and the whole of mankind was
turned to clay ; like reeds the corpses floated. I opened
the window, and the light smote upon my face ; I
stooped and sat down ; I weep, over my face flow my
tears. I watch the regions at the edge of the sea ; a
district rose twelve measures high. To the land of
Nizir steered the ship ; the mountain of Nizir stopped
the ship, and it was not able to pass over it. The first
day, the second day, the mountain of Nizir stopped the
ship. The third day, the fourth day, the mountain of
Nizir stopped the ship. The fifth day, the sixth day,
the mountain of Nizir stopped the ship. The seventh
day when it approached I sent forth a dove, and it left.
The dove went and returned, and found no resting-place,
and it came back. Then I sent forth a swallow, and it
left. The swallow went and returned, and found no
resting-place, and it came back. I sent forth a raven,
and it left. The raven went and saw the carrion on the
water, and it ate, it swam, it wandered away ; it did not
return. I sent (the animals) forth to the four winds, I

sacrificed a sacrifice. I built an altar on the peak of the mountain. I set vessels [each containing the third of an ephah] by sevens; underneath them I spread reeds, pine-wood, and spices. The gods smelt the savour; the gods smelt the good savour; the gods gathered like flies over the sacrifices. Thereupon the great goddess at her approach lighted up the rainbow which Anu had created according to his glory. The crystal brilliance of those gods before me may I not forget;

(Col. IV) those days I have thought of, and never may I forget them. May the gods come to my altar; but may Bel not come to my altar, since he did not consider but caused the flood, and my people he assigned to the abyss. When thereupon Bel at his approach saw the ship, Bel stopped; he was filled with anger against the gods and the spirits of heaven: 'Let none come forth alive! let no man live in the abyss!' Adar opened his mouth and spake, he says to the warrior Bel: 'Who except Ea can form a design? Yea, Ea knows, and all things he communicates.' Ea opened his mouth and spake, he says to the warrior Bel: 'Thou, O warrior prince of the gods, why, why didst thou not consider but causedst a flood? Let the doer of sin bear his sin, let the doer of wickedness bear his wickedness. May the just prince not be cut off, may the faithful not be (destroyed). Instead of causing a flood, let lions increase, that men may be minished; instead of causing a flood, let hyænas increase, that men may be minished; instead of causing a flood, let a famine happen, that men may be (wasted); instead of causing a flood, let plague increase, that men may be (reduced). I did not reveal the determination of the great gods To Sisuthros alone a dream I sent, and he heard the

determination of the gods.'   When Bel had again taken
counsel with himself, he went up into the midst of the
ship.   He took my hand and bid me ascend, even me
he bid ascend ; he united my wife to my side ; he turned
himself to us and joined himself to us in covenant ; he
blesses us (thus) : ' Hitherto Sisuthros has been a mortal
man, but now Sisuthros and his wife are united together
in being raised to be like the gods ; yea, Sisuthros shall
dwell afar off at the mouth of the rivers.'   They took
me, and afar off at the mouth of the rivers they made
me dwell."

It is hardly necessary to indicate the points of agreement and disagreement between this Babylonian account
of the Deluge and that of Genesis.   The most striking
difference between the two, that which first meets the eye,
is the polytheism of the Babylonian version, in contrast
with the monotheism of the Biblical narrative.   Here,
in place of the gods of Chaldea, we are confronted by
the one supreme Deity ; we have no longer to do with a
Bel who requires the intercession of Ea before he will
consent not to destroy the guiltless with the guilty ; it
is the Lord Himself who " said in His heart, I will not
again curse the ground any more for man's sake."   In
the Babylonian legend, moreover, Noah and Enoch
have been confounded together ; Sisuthros is not only
saved from the waters of the flood, but translated to the
abode of the gods.   The vessel itself in which the seed
of life was preserved is not the same in the two accounts.
According to the Hebrew narrative, it was an ark ;
according to the Babylonian poem, a ship.   It is true
that in one place it is called " a palace," the word used
being the same as that which in many passages of the
Old Testament is applied to God's " palace " of heaven ;

but it is provided with a pilot, Buzur-sadi-rabi, "the Sun-god of the mighty mountain," and Sisuthros is made to expostulate on the strangeness of building a ship which should sail over the land. It must, however, be noticed that the shrines in which the images of the gods were carried in Babylonia were called "ships," and that these "ships" corresponded with the ark of the Hebrew tabernacle.

The land of Nizir, in which the vessel of Sisuthros rested, was among the mountains of Pir Mam, to the north-east of Babylonia. Rowandiz, the highest peak in this part of Asia, rises a little to the north of the Pir Mam, and it seems probable, therefore, that it represents " the mountain of Nizir." The whole country had been included by the Accadians in the vast territory of Guti, or Gutium, which roughly corresponds with the modern Kurdistan. It is accordingly worth notice that a wide-spread eastern tradition makes Gebel Gudi, or Mount Gudi, the mountain on which the ark rested, and that in early Jewish legend this mountain is called Lubar or Baris, the boundary between Armenia and Kurdistan, in the land of the Minni. Ararat, or Urardhu, as it is written in the cuneiform inscriptions, denoted Armenia, and more particularly the district about Lake Van ; so that "the mountains of Ararat," of which Genesis speaks, might easily have been the Kurdish ranges of Southern Armenia. It was not until a very late period that the name of Ararat was first applied and then confined to the lofty mountains in the north.

Rowandiz seems also to have been regarded in Acca-dian mythology as the Olympos on which the gods dwelt. In this case it was usually called "the mountain of the east ; " but the east was here the north-east, since

other legends identified it with Aralu, or Hades, the
mountain of gold which was fabled to be in the far
north.   It is to this Accadian Olympos that reference is
made in Isa. xiv. 13, where the King of Babylon is
described as boasting that he would "ascend into heaven,
and exalt his throne above the stars of the gods," that
he would "sit on the mountain of the assembly of the
gods in the extremities of the north."   The mountain
was sometimes known as the "mountain of the world,"
since the firmament was supposed to revolve on its peak
as on a pivot.   We must not imagine, however, that the
Accadians, any more than the Greeks, actually believed
the gods to live above the clouds on the terrestrial
Rowandiz, except at a very early period in their history.
Just as we do not think of the sky when we use the
word heaven in a spiritual sense, so by "the mountain
of the assembly of the gods" they meant a spiritual
mountain, of which Rowandiz was the earthly type.   It
is in this way that we must explain the position
assigned to Sisuthros after his translation.   He does not
live along with the gods in the north, but has his station
fixed "at the mouth of the rivers" Euphrates and
Tigris, which in ancient times flowed into the Persian
Gulf through separate channels.   At an epoch when
the geographical knowledge of the Accadians did not
extend very far, the unknown district beyond the
mouth of the Euphrates became a representative of the
other world ; and the Euphrates itself was identified
with Datilla, the river of "the God of life and death,"
as well as with the stream or "great deep" which was
supposed to encircle the earth like a monstrous
serpent.

The name of the Chaldean Noah, Sisuthros, or, as it

is written in the cuneiform, Khasis-adra, or Adra-khasis, is really a title, given to him on account of his righteousness, and signifying "wise (and) pious." His proper name is one which means "the Sun of Life," though the exact pronunciation of it is somewhat uncertain. Neither of these names agrees with that of the Biblical Noah, but the latter has received a full explanation from the Assyrian language, where it signifies "rest."

After the Flood, we are told in Genesis that men journeyed from the east until they came to the plain of Shinar, where they built the tower of Babel, in the vain hope of ascending into heaven. God, however, confounded their language and scattered them over the face of the earth. The references in this narrative to Shinar and Babel, or Babylon, indicate that here again we may expect to find a Babylonian account of the Confusion of Tongues, just as we have found a Babylonian account of the Deluge. As we have seen, the Accadians regarded themselves as having come from the "mountain of the east" where the ark had rested, while Shinar is the Hebrew form of the native name Sumir—or Sungir, as it was pronounced in the allied dialect of Accad— the southern half of pre-Semitic Babylonia. Now Mr. George Smith discovered some broken fragments of a cuneiform text which evidently related to the building of the Tower of Babel. It tells us how certain men had "turned against the father of all the gods," and how the thoughts of their leader's heart "were evil." At Babylon they essayed to build "a mound" or hill-like tower, but the winds blew down their work, and Anu "confounded great and small on the mound," as well as their "speech," and "made strange their counsel." The very word that is used in the sense of "confounding" in the narrative of Genesis is used also in the Assyrian text. The Biblical writer, by a play upon words, not uncommon in the Old Testament, compares it with the name of Babel, though etymologically the latter word has nothing to do with it. Babel is the Assyrian Bab-ili, "Gate of God," and is merely a Semitic translation of the old Accadian (or rather Sumirian) name of the town, Ca-dimíra, where Ca is "gate" and dimíra "God." Chaldean tradition assigned the construction of the tower and the consequent confusion of languages to the time of the autumnal equinox ; and it is possible that the hero-king Etanna (Titan in Greek writers), who is stated to have built a city in defiance of the will of heaven, was the wicked chief under whom the tower was raised.

The confusion of tongues was followed by the dispersion of mankind. The earth was again peopled by the descendants of the three sons of Noah—Shem, Ham, and Japhet. Shem is the Assyrian Samu, "olive-coloured," Ham is Khammu, "burned black," and Japhet Ippat, "the white race." The tribes and races which drew their origin from them are enumerated in the tenth chapter of Genesis. The arrangement of this chapter, however, is geographical, not ethnological ; the peoples named in it being grouped together according to their geographical position, not according to their relationship in blood or language. Here it is that the non-Semitic Elamites are classed along with the Semitic Assyrians, and that the Phœnicians of Canaan, who spoke the same language as the Hebrews, and originally came from the same ancestors, are associated with the Egyptians. When this fact is recognised, there is no difficulty in showing that the statements of the chapter are fully consistent with the conclusions of modern research.

The Assyrian inscriptions have thrown a good deal of light upon the names contained in it. Gomer, the son of Japhet, represents the Gimirrai of the inscriptions, the Kimmerians of classical writers. Pressed by the Scyths of the Russian steppes, they threatened to overrun the Assyrian empire under a leader named Teispes, but were defeated by Esar-haddon, in B.C. 670, in a great battle on the north-eastern frontier of his kingdom, and driven westwards into Asia Minor. There they sacked the Greek town of Sinôpê, and spread like locusts over the fertile plains of Lydia. Among the gifts sent to Nineveh by the Lydian king, Gugu or Gygès—a name in which we may see the Gog of Ezekiel—were two Kimmerian chieftains whom he had captured with his own hand. Gyges was afterwards slain in battle with the barbarians, and it required some years before they could be finally extirpated.

Madai are the Medes, a title given by the Assyrians to the multifarious tribes to the east of Kurdistan. They are first mentioned in the inscriptions about 820 B.C., and were partially subdued by Tiglath-Pileser II and his successors. At this time they lived in independent communities, each governed by its "city-chief." The Median empire, which rose upon the ruins of Nineveh, was really the creation of the kings of Ekbatana, the modern Hamadan. The population of this district was known among the Babylonians as *manda*, or "barbarians;" and through a confusion of the latter word with the proper name Madâ, or "Medes," historians have been led to suppose that the empire of Ekbatana was a Median one.

Javan is the Greek word "Ionian," but in the Old Testament it is generally applied to the island of

Cyprus, which is called the Island of Yavnan, or the
Ionians, on the Assyrian monuments. A more specific
name for it in Hebrew is Kittim, derived from the name
of the Phœnician colony of Kition, now represented by
Larnaka. Cyprus was first visited by the Babylonians
at a very remote period, since Sargon I of Accad, who,
according to Nabonidos (B.C. 550), lived 3,200 years
before his time, carried his arms as far as its shores.
As for Tubal and Meshech, they are as frequently
associated together in the Assyrian inscriptions as they
are in the Bible. The Tubal or Tibarêni spread in Old
Testament times over the south-eastern part of Kappadokia, while the Meshech or Moschi adjoined them
on the north and west. Ashkenaz is the Assyrian
Asguza, the name of a district which lay between the
kingdoms of Ekbatana and the Minni.

Cush and Mizraim denote Ethiopia and Egypt,
Ethiopia roughly corresponding to the Nubia of to-
day. As Ethiopia was largely peopled by tribes who
had come across the Red Sea from Southern Arabia,
the name of Cush was given in the Old Testament
(as in verse 7 of this chapter) to Southern Arabia
also. Properly speaking, however, it denoted the
country which commenced on the southern side of the
First Cataract. Mizraim means "the two Matsors,"
that is Upper and Lower Egypt. Lower Egypt was
the original Matsor, a word which signifies "wall," and
referred to the line of fortification which defended the
kingdom on the eastern side from the attacks of
Asiatic tribes. The word occurs more than once in the
Biblical writers, though its sense has been obscured in
the Authorised Version. Thus in Isaiah xxxvii. 25,
Sennacherib boasts that he has "dried up all the rivers

of Matsor," that is to say, the mouths of the Nile ; and in
Isaiah xix. 6, we ought to translate "the Nile-arms of
Matsor," instead of "brooks of defence." While Matsor
was the name of Lower Egypt, Upper Egypt was termed
Pathros (Isa. xi. 11), which is the Egyptian Pe-to-res
or "southern land." The Pathrusim or inhabitants of
Pathros are mentioned among the sons of Mizraim in
the chapter of Genesis upon which we are engaged.

Phut seems to be the Egyptian Punt, on the Somali
coast. Spices and other precious objects of merchan-
dise were brought from it, and the Egyptians sometimes
called it "the divine land." The Lehabim of verse 13
are the Libyans, while the Naphtuhim may be the
people of Napata in Ethiopia. The Caphtorim or
inhabitants of Caphtor are the Phœnician population
settled on the coast of the Delta. From an early period
the whole of this district had been colonised by the
Phœnicians, and, as Phœnicia itself was called Keft by
the Egyptians, the part of Egypt in which they had
settled went by the name of Keft-ur or "greater
Phœnicia." From various passages of the Old Testament[1] we learn that the Philistines, whom the kings of
Egypt had once employed to garrison the five cities in
the extreme south of Palestine, had originally been
Phœnicians of Caphtor, so that the words of the verse
before us must have been moved from their proper
place, "Caphtorim, out of whom came Philistim," being
the correct reading.

Canaan signifies "the lowlands," and was primarily
the name of the coast on which the great cities of
Phœnicia were built. As, however, the inland parts of
the country were inhabited by a kindred population, the

[1] Deut. ii. 23, Jer. xlvii. 4, Amos ix. 7.

name came to be extended to designate the whole of
Palestine, just as Palestine itself meant originally only
the small territory of the Philistines. In Isaiah's prophecy upon Tyre (xxiii. 11) the word is used in its
primitive sense, though here again the Authorised
Version has misled the English reader by mistranslating
" the merchant-city" instead of "Canaan." Sidon,
"the fishers' town," was the oldest of the Canaanite or
Phœnician cities ; like Tyre, it was divided into two
quarters, known respectively as Greater and Lesser
Sidon. Heth or the Hithites adjoined the Phœnicians
on the north ; we shall have a good deal to say about
them in a future chapter, and therefore pass them by
now. The Amorite was the inhabitant of the mountains
of Palestine, in contrast to the Canaanite or lowlander,
and the name is met with on the Egyptian monuments.
The towns of Arka and Simirra (or Zemar) are both
mentioned by Tiglath-Pileser II, while the city of Arvad
or Arados (now Ruâd) is repeatedly named in the
Assyrian inscriptions. So also is Hamath (now Hamah),
which was conquered by Sargon, and made by him the
seat of an Assyrian governor.

The name of Elam has first received its explanation
from the decipherment of the Assyrian texts. It was
the name of the mountainous region to the east of
Babylonia, of which Shushan or Susa was at one time
the capital, and is nothing more than the Assyrian word
elam, "high." *Elam* was itself a translation of the
Accadian *Numma*, under which the Accadians included
the whole of the highlands which bounded the plain
of Babylonia on its eastern side. It was the seat of
an ancient monarchy which rivalled in antiquity that
of Chaldea itself, and was long a dangerous neighbour

to the latter. It was finally overthrown, however, by Assur-bani-pal, the Assyrian king, about B.C. 645. The native title of the country was Anzan or Ansan, and the name of its capital, Susan or Shushan, seems to have signified "the old town" in the language of its inhabitants.

Asshur or Assur was originally the name of a city on the banks of the Tigris, the ruins of which are now known as Kalah Sherghat. The name was of Accadian derivation, and signified "water-bank." The city long continued to be the capital of the district which was called after it Assyria, but was eventually supplanted by Ninua or Nineveh. Nineveh lay opposite the present town of Mosul, and it is from the remains of its chief palace, now buried under the mounds of Kouyunjik, that most of the Assyrian inscriptions in the British Museum have been brought. A few miles to the south of Nineveh, on the site now known as Nimrûd, was Calah, a town built by Shalmaneser I, who lived B.C. 1300. Calah subsequently fell into ruins, but was rebuilt in the ninth century before our era. "Between Nineveh and Calah" stood Resen, according to Genesis. Resen is the Assyrian *Ris-eni*, "head of the stream," which is once mentioned in an inscription of Senna-cherib. Rehoboth 'Ir, or "the open spaces of the city," must have denoted the suburbs of Nineveh, and cannot be identified with Dur-Sarrukin, founded by Sargon at Khorsabad, several miles to the north.

It is plain from the context that Arphaxad must signify Chaldea; and this conclusion is verified by the fact that the name might also be pronounced Arpa-Chesed, or "border of Chaldæa." Chesed is the singular of Casdim, the word used in the Old Testament to

denote the inhabitants of Babylonia. The origin of it
is doubtful, but, as has been suggested above, it most
probably represents the Assyrian *casidi*, "conquerors,"
a term which might very well be applied to the
Semitic conquerors of Sumir and Accad. The Greek
word Chaldeans is derived from the Kaldâ, a tribe
which lived on the shores of the Persian Gulf, and is
first heard of in the ninth century before our era. Under
Merodach-Baladan, the Kaldâ made themselves masters
of Babylonia, and became so integral a part of the
population as to give their name to the whole of it in
classical times.

Aram, the brother of Arphaxad, represents, of course,
the Aramæans of Aram, or "the highlands," which
included the greater part of Mesopotamia and Syria.
In the later days of the Assyrian Empire, Aramaic, the
language of Aram, became the common language of
trade and diplomacy, which every merchant and politician was supposed to learn, and in still later times
succeeded in supplanting Assyrian in Assyria and
Babylonia, as well as Hebrew in Palestine, until in its
turn it was supplanted by Arabic.

Lud seems to be a misreading; at all events, Lydia
and the Lydians, on the extreme western coast of Asia
Minor, had nothing to do with the peoples of Elam,
of Assyria, and of Aram. What the original reading
was, however, it is now impossible to say.

In the midst of all these geographical names we find
a notice inserted relating to "the mighty hunter"
Nimrod, the beginning of whose kingdom, we are told,
was Babylon, and Erech, and Accad, and Calneh in the
land of Shinar. His name has not yet been discovered
in the cuneiform records. Some Assyrian scholars have

wished to identify him with Gisdhubar, the hero of the great Chaldean epic, which contains the account of the Deluge; but Gisdhubar was a solar hero who had originally been the Accadian god of fire. It is true that Gisdhubar was the special deity of the town of Marad, and that Na-Marad would signify in the Accadian language " the prince of Marad "; such a title, however, has not been found in the inscriptions. Erech, called Uruk on the monuments, is now represented by the mounds of Warka, far away to the south of Babylon, and was one of the oldest and most important of the Babylonian cities. Like Calneh, the Kul-unu of the monuments, it was situated in the division of the country known as Sumir or Shinar. Accad, from which the northern division of the country took its name, was a suburb of Sippara (now Abu-Habba), and, along with the latter, made up the Sepharvaim or " Two Sipparas" of Scripture. The Accadian form of the name was Agadê, and here was the seat of a great library formed in remote days by Sargon I, and containing, among other treasures, a work on astronomy and astrology in seventy-two books.

The translation of the verse which follows the list of Nimrod's Babylonian cities is doubtful. It is a question whether we should render with the Authorised Version : " Out of that land went forth Asshur," or prefer the alternative translation : " Out of that land he went forth to Assyria." The latter is favoured by Micah v. 6, where " the land of Nimrod " appears to mean Assyria. But the question cannot be finally decided until we discover some positive information about Nimrod on the monuments.

If, however, little light has been thrown by modern

research on the person of Nimrod, this is by no means
the case as regards Abraham. Abu-ramu or Abram,
"the exalted father," Abraham's original name, is a
name which also occurs on early Babylonian contract-
tablets. Sarah, again, is the Assyrian *sarrat*, "queen,"
while Milcah, the daughter of Haran, is the Assyrian
milcat, "princess." The site of Ur of the Chaldees, the
birthplace of Abram, has been discovered, and excavations have been made among the ruins of its temples.
The site is now called Mugheir, and lies on the western
side of the Euphrates, on the border of the desert,
immediately to the west of Erech. The chief temple of
Ur was dedicated to the moon-god, and the Accadian
inscriptions on its bricks, which record its foundation, are
among the earliest that we possess. It was, in fact, the
capital of one of the oldest of the pre-Semitic dynasties,
and its very name, Uru or Ur, is only the Semitic form
of the Accadian *eri*, "city." It is probable that it had
passed into the hands of the Semitic "Casdim" before
the age of Abraham ; at all events, it had long been the
resort of Semitic traders, who had ceased to lead the
roving life of their ancestors in the Arabian desert.
From Ur, Abraham's father had migrated to Haran, in
the northern part of Mesopotamia, on the high road
which led from Babylonia and Assyria into Syria and
Palestine. Why he should have migrated to so distant
a city has been a great puzzle, and has tempted scholars
to place both Ur and Haran in wrong localities ; but
here, again, the cuneiform inscriptions have at last
furnished us with the key. As far back as the Accadian
epoch, the district in which Haran was built belonged
to the rulers of Babylonia ; Haran was, in fact, the
frontier town of the empire, commanding at once the

highway into the west and the fords of the Euphrates; the name itself was an Accadian one signifying "the road"; and the deity to whom it was dedicated was the moon-god of Ur. The symbol of this deity was a conical stone, with a star above it, and gems with this symbol engraved upon them may be seen in the British Museum.

The road which passed through Haran was well known to the Chaldean kings and their subjects. Sargon I of Accad, and his son Naram-Sin, had already made expeditions into the far west. Sargon had carved his image on the rocks of the Mediterranean coast, and had even crossed over into the island of Cyprus. The campaign, therefore, of Chedor-laomer and his allies, recorded in the fourteenth chapter of Genesis, was no new thing. The soil of Canaan had already felt the tramp of Babylonian feet. We can even fix the approximate date at which the campaign took place, and when Abraham and his confederates surprised the invaders and recovered from them the spoils of Southern Palestine. For twelve years, we are told, the tribes in the neighbourhood of the Dead Sea had served Chedor-laomer, king of Elam, and then they rebelled; but the rebellion was quickly followed by invasion. Chedor-laomer and "the kings that were with him,"—Amraphel, king of Shinar, Arioch, king of Ellasar, and Tidal, "king of nations,"—marched against the revolters, overthrew them in battle, and carried them away captive. The name of Arioch is actually found on the cuneiform monuments. Bricks have been discovered engraved with the legend of Eri-aku, king of Larsa, the son of Kudur-Mabug the Elamite. Eri-aku means in Accadian "the servant of the moon-god," and Larsa, his capital, is now represented by the mounds of Senkereh, a little to the east of Erech. Kudur-Mabug is entitled "the father of Palestine," and it would, therefore, seem that he claimed supremacy over Canaan. His name is an Elamite one, signifying "the servant of the god Mabug," and is closely parallel to the Biblical Chedor-laomer, that is, Kudur-Lagamar, "the servant of the god Lagamar." Lagamar and Mabug, however, were different deities, and we cannot, therefore, identify Chedor-laomer and Kudur-Mabug together. But it is highly probable that they were brothers, Chedor-laomer being the elder, who held sway in Elam, while his nephew Eri-aku owned allegiance to him in Southern Babylonia. At any rate, it is plain from the history of Genesis that Babylon was at this time subject to Elam, and under the government of more than one ruler. Amraphel would have been king of that portion of Sumir, or Southern Chaldea, which was not comprised in the dominions of the king of Larsa ; and the fact that the narrative begins by stating that the campaign in Palestine was made in his days, seems to imply that the whole account has been extracted from the Babylonian archives. As for "Tidal, king of nations," it is very possible that we ought to read Turgal (Thorgal), with the Septuagint, while Goyyim or "nations" has been shown by Sir Henry Rawlinson to be a misreading for Gutium, the name given to the tract of country northward of Babylonia, which stretched from Mesopotamia to the mountains of Kurdistan, and within which the kingdom of Assyria afterwards arose.

Now, the Assyrian king Assur-bani-pal tells us that an image of the goddess Nana had been carried away from Babylonia by the Elamite king Kudur-Nankhundi when he overran Chaldea 1635 years before his own time, that is to say, in 2280 B.C. It is possible that this invasion of the country by Kudur-Nankhundi was the beginning of Elamite supremacy in Babylonia, and that Kudur-Mabug and Chedor-laomer were descendants of his. If so, we shall have an approximate date for the rescue of Lot by Abraham, and consequently for the age of Abraham himself.

The fourteenth chapter of Genesis is the last in the Book that relates to Babylonia. The history now turns to Egypt; and it is, therefore, from the monuments of Egypt, and not from those of Babylonia and Assyria, that we henceforth have to look for light and information.

No traditions of a deluge had been preserved among the Egyptians. They believed, however, that there was a time when the greater part of mankind had been destroyed by the angry gods. A myth told how men had once uttered hostile words against their creator Ra, the Sun-God, who accordingly sent the goddess Hathor to slay them, so that the earth was covered with their blood as far as the town of Herakleopolis. Then Ra drank 7,000 cups of wine, made from the fruits of Egypt and mingled with the blood of the slain; his heart rejoiced, and he made an oath that he would not destroy mankind again. Rain filled the wells, and Ra went forth to fight against his human foes. Their bows were broken and themselves slaughtered, and the god returned victorious to heaven, where he created Paradise and the people of the stars. This myth agrees with another, according to which mankind had emanated from the eyes of Ra, though there was a different legend of the creation, which asserted that all men, with the exception of the negroes, had sprung from the tears of the two deities Horus and Sekhet.

D

When Abraham went down into Egypt the empire
was already very old. Its history begins with Menes,
who united the independent states of the Nile valley
into a single kingdom, and established his capital at
Memphis. The first six dynasties of kings, who reigned
1,478 years, represent what is called the Old Empire. It
was under the monarchs of the fourth dynasty that the
pyramids of Gizeh were built ; and at no time during its
later history did the art and culture of Egypt reach
again so high a level as it did under the Old Empire.
With the close of the sixth dynasty came a period of
disaster and decline. When Egypt again emerged into
the light of history it was under the warrior princes of
the twelfth dynasty. The capital had been shifted to
the new city of Thebes, in the south, a new god, Amun,
presided over the Egyptian deities, and the ruling class
itself differed in blood and features from the men of the
Old Empire. Henceforth Egyptian art was characterised
by a stiff conventionality wholly unlike the freedom and
vigour of the art of the early dynasties; the government became more autocratic ; and the obelisk took the
place of the pyramid in architecture. But the Middle
Empire, as it has been termed, did not last long.
Semitic invaders from Canaan and Arabia overran the
country, and established their seat at Zoan or Tanis.
For 511 years they held the Egyptians in bondage,
though the native princes, who had taken refuge in the
south, gradually acquired more and more power, until at
last, under the leadership of Aahmes or Amosis, the
founder of the eighteenth dynasty, they succeeded in
driving the hated foreigners out. These foreigners are
known to history as the Hyksos or Shepherds, Hyksos
being the Egyptian *hik shasu*, " prince of the Shasu," or

"Beduins." The name which they bear upon the monuments is Menti.

It must have been while the Hyksos monarchs were holding their court at Zoan that Abraham entered the land. He found there men of Semitic blood, like himself, and speaking a Semitic language. A welcome was assured him, and he had no need of an interpreter. But the Hyksos kings had already begun to assume Egyptian state and to adopt Egyptian customs. In place of the Semitic *shalat*, "ruler," the title by which their first leaders had been known, they had borrowed the Egyptian title of Pharaoh. Pharaoh appears on the monuments as *pir-aa*, "great house," the palace in which the king lived being used to denote the king himself, just as in our own time the "porte" or gate of the palace has become synonymous with the Turkish Sultan.

By the time that Joseph was sold into Egypt there was little outward difference between the court at Zoan and the court of the native princes at Thebes. The very names and titles borne by the Hyksos officials had become Egyptian; and though they still regarded the god Set as the chief object of their worship, they had begun to rebuild the Egyptian temples, and pay honour to the Egyptian deities. Potiphar, to whom Joseph was sold, bore a purely Egyptian name, meaning "the gift of the risen one," while the name of Potipherah, the high priest of On, whose daughter, Asenath, was married by Joseph, is equally Egyptian, and signifies "the gift of the Sun-God." The Sun-God was the special deity of On; to him the great temple of the city was dedicated, and the name by which the place was known to the Greeks was Heliopolis, "the city of the sun." It was the city whose name is played upon in Isaiah xix. 18, where the prophet declares that in the day when Egypt shall be converted to the Lord, "the City of the Sun" (*'ir ha-kheres*) shall become "the city of the destruction" of idols (*'ir ha-heres*). Jeremiah, too, plays similarly upon the name, when he says that Nebuchadnezzar, "shall break also the images of Beth-Shemesh (the house of the Sun-God) that is in the land of Egypt" (Jer. xliii. 13); while Ezekiel changes the Egyptian word On into the Hebrew *aven*, "nothingness," and prophesies that "the young men of Aven shall fall by the sword" (Ezek. xxx. 17). The ruins of On are within an afternoon's drive of Cairo : but nothing remains of the city except mounds of earth, and a solitary obelisk that once stood in front of the great temple of the sun, and had been reared by Usertasen I, of the twelfth dynasty, a thousand years before the daughter of its priest became the wife of Joseph. The name of this daughter, Asenath, is the Egyptian 'Snat.

We are told that when the Pharaoh had made Joseph "ruler over all the land of Egypt" he gave him a new name, Zaphnath-paaneah (Gen. xli. 45). According to Dr. Brugsch, this name is the Egyptian *Za pa-u nt pa-aa-ankh*, "governor of the district of the place of life," that is, of the district in which the Israelites afterwards built the towns of Raamses and Pithom, and in which the land of Goshen seems to have been situated. In after times Egyptian legend confounded Joseph with Moses, and changing the divine name which formed the first element in his into that of the Egyptian god Osiris, called him Osar-siph. The Jewish historian, Josephus, has preserved for us the story which made Osar-siph the leader of the Israelites in their flight from Egypt.

The seven years' famine, which Joseph predicted, is a

rare occurrence in Egypt. In a country where rain is
almost unknown, the fertility of the fields depends upon
the annual inundation of the Nile when swollen by the
melting snows of Abyssinia. It is only where the
waters can penetrate, or can be led by canals and
irrigating machines, that the soil is capable of supporting
vegetation ; but wherever this takes place the mud they
bring with them is so fertilising that the peasantry
frequently grow three luxuriant crops on the same piece
of ground during the same year. For the inundation to
fail in any single year is not common ; for it to fail
seven years running is a most unusual event. The last
recorded time when there was a seven years' failure of
the river, and a consequent famine, was in A.D. 1064—
1071, under the reign of the Khalif El-Mustansir Billah.
A similar failure must have taken place in the age of
the twelfth dynasty, since Ameni, an officer of King
Usurtasen I, who has engraved the history of his life at
the entrance of his tomb among the cliffs of Beni-
Hassan, states that "no one was hungry in my days,
not even in the years of famine. For I had tilled all
the fields of the district of Mah, up to the southern and
northern frontiers. Thus I prolonged the life of its
inhabitants, and preserved the food which it produced.
No hungry man was in it. I distributed equally to the
widow as to the married woman. I did not prefer the
great to the humble in all that I gave away."[1]

Another long famine of the same kind happened at a
later date, and may possibly be that against which
Joseph provided in Northern Egypt. The sepulchral
tablet of a nobleman, called Baba, far away at El-Kab
in Southern Egypt, informs us of the fact. In this the

[1] Brugsch, "History of Egypt" (Eng. Tr.), I, p. 158.

dead man is made to say : "When a famine arose,
lasting many years, I distributed corn to the city each
year of famine."

Baba is supposed to have lived shortly before the
establishment of the eighteenth dynasty; and this
would agree very well with the date which we must
assign to Joseph. As we shall see in the next chapter,
we now know the exact period of Egyptian history at
which the Exodus must have taken place ; and if we
count 430 years, "the sojourning of the children of Israel
who dwelt in Egypt" (Exod. xii. 40), back from this,
we shall be brought to the reign of the Hyksos king
Apophis or Apepi, the very king, in fact, under whom,
according to ancient authors, Joseph was raised to be
the *adon*, or second ruler of the state. It was not until
the Hyksos were driven out of the country, and Aahmes,
the founder of the eighteenth dynasty, was pursuing with
bitter hatred both them and their friends that "there
arose up a new king over Egypt, which knew not Joseph."

The earlier history of Joseph in the house of Potiphar
finds a curious parallel in an old Egyptian romance,
known as the Tale of the Two Brothers, which was composed by a scribe named Enna in the thirteenth century
B.C. Anepu, it is there said, sent his younger brother,
Bata, from the field where they were working, to fetch
corn from the village. "And the young brother found
the wife of his elder brother occupied in braiding her
hair. And he said to her, 'Rise up, give me seed-corn,
that I may return to the field, for thus has my elder
brother enjoined me, to return without delay.' The
woman said to him, 'Go in, open the chest, that thou
mayest take what thine heart desires, otherwise my
locks will fall by the way.' And the youth entered

into the stable, and took thereout a large vessel, for it
was his wish to carry away much seed-corn. And he
loaded himself with wheat and grains of durra, and went
out with it.   Then she said unto him, 'How great is the
burden on thine arm?'   He said to her, 'Two measures
of durra and three measures of wheat, making together
five measures, which rest on my arms.'   Thus he spake
to her.   But she spake to the youth and said, 'How
great is thy strength!   Well have I remarked thy
vigour every time.'   And her heart knew him! . . . .
And she stood up and laid hold of him, and she said
to him, 'Come, let us enjoy an hour's rest.   The most
beautiful things shall be thy portion, for I will prepare
for thee festal garments.'   Then the youth became like
the panther of the south for rage, on account of the
evil word which she had spoken to him ; but she was
afraid beyond all measure.   And he spoke to her and
said, 'Thou, O woman, hast been to me like a mother,
and thy husband like a father, for he is older than I, so
that he might have been my parent.   Why this so great
sin, that thou hast spoken to me?   Say it not to me
another time, then will I not tell it this time, and no
word of it shall come out of my mouth about it to any
man whatsoever.'   And he loaded himself with his
burden, and went out into the field.   And he went to
his elder brother, and they completed their day's work.
When it was now evening, the elder brother returned
home to his dwelling.   And his young brother followed
behind his oxen, which he had laden with all the good
things of the field, driving them before him, to prepare
for their resting-place in the stable in the village.   And,
behold, the wife of his elder brother was afraid because
of the word which she had spoken, and she took a jar of

fat, and she made herself like one to whom an evil-doer had offered violence. She wished thereby to say to her husband, 'Thy young brother has offered me violence.' And her husband returned home at evening, according to his daily custom, and entered into his house,.and found his wife stretched out and suffering from injury. She gave him no water for his hands, according to her custom. And the lamp was not lighted, so that the house was in darkness. But she lay there and vomited. And her husband spoke to her thus, 'Who has had to do with thee? Lift thyself up!' She said to him, 'No one has had to do with me except thy young brother; for when he came to take seed-corn for thee, he found me sitting alone, and he said to me, 'Come, let us make merry an hour and rest! Let down thy hair!' Thus he spake to me; but I did not listen to him (but said), 'See, am I not thy mother, and is not thy elder brother like a father to thee?' Thus I spoke to him; but he did not hearken to my speech, and used force with me, that I might not make a report to thee. Now, if thou allowest him to live, I will kill myself." [1]   Anepu then took a knife, and went out to kill his brother. The cows, however, warned Bata of his danger, and the Sun-god came to his aid, and set a river full of crocodiles between himself and Anepu. When Anepu eventually learned the real truth, he hurried back to his house, and put his wife to death.

No name like that of Goshen, where the Israelites were settled by order of the Pharaoh, has as yet been discovered upon the monuments. Goshen, however, could not have been far from the north-eastern frontier

[1] Brugsch, " History of Egypt" (Eng. Tr.), I. pp. 309-311.

of Egypt, and from Genesis xlvii. 11, we learn that it was in the land of Rameses. Now, Dr. Brugsch has shown that Ramses, or Rameses, was the title given to Zoan by Ramses II, when he raised it anew from the ruins in which it had lain since the expulsion of the Hyksos, and filled it again with stately edifices. Goshen consequently must have been in the neighbourhood of Zoan, as, indeed, we might expect, since Joseph's family would naturally be settled not far from the capital and the residence of the powerful minister. It was from hence that Jacob's body, after being embalmed, as was customary in Egypt, was carried to the old family tomb at Hebron; and we can therefore understand why Zoan and Hebron were brought into such close relation in the well-known passage of Numbers (xiii. 22) where it is said that "Hebron was built seven years before Zoan in Egypt." Hebron and Zoan were the two points around which centred the patriarchal history which is set before us in the Book of Genesis.

CHAPTER III.

THE EXODUS OUT OF EGYPT.

Egypt during the sojourn of the Israelites.—The travels of an Egyptian officer through Palestine before the time of Joshua.—Recent excavations at Tel el-Maskhûta.—Discovery of the treasure-chambers built by the Israelites. —Date of the Exodus fixed.—Origin of the word Jehovah.—The rite of circumcision.—Origin of the name Moses.—Illustrations of Hebrew law and ritual from Phœnician and Assyrian monuments.—Tablet describing the duties of a priest of Bel.—The sacrificial tariff of Marseilles.— Phœnician texts found in Cyprus.

THE expulsion of the Hyksos conquerors of Egypt, while it brought oppression and slavery to their Semitic kindred who were left behind, inaugurated an era of conquest and glory for the Egyptians themselves. The war against the Asiatics which had begun in Egypt was carried into Asia, and under Thothmes III and other great monarchs of the eighteenth dynasty the Egyptian armies traversed Palestine and Syria, and penetrated as far as the Euphrates. The tribes of Canaan paid tribute ; the Amorites or "hill-men" were led into captivity ; and the combined armies of Hittites and Phœnicians were defeated in the plain of Megiddo. On the temple-walls of Karnak at Thebes, Thothmes III (B.C. 1600) gives a list of the Canaanitish towns which had submitted to his arms. Among them we read the names of Zarthan and Beroth, of Beth-Anoth and Gibeah, of Migdol and Ophrah, of Taanach and Jibleam, of Shunem and Chinneroth, of Hazor and Laish, of Merom and Kishon, of Abel and Sharon, of Joppa and Achzib, of Beyrut and Accho, of

Heshbon and Megiddo, of Hamath and Damascus. One of the conquered places bears the curious name of Jacob-el, "Jacob the God," while mention is made of the Negeb, or "southern district," which afterwards formed part of the territory of Judah.

Two centuries later, when the troublous times which saw the close of the eighteenth dynasty had ushered in the nineteenth, the same districts had again to be overrun by the Egyptian kings. Once more victories were gained over the powerful Hittites, in their fortress of Kadesh, on the Orontes, and over the tribes of Palestine. Seti I, the father of Ramses II, records among his conquests Beth-Anoth and Kirjath-Anab[1] in the south, as well as Zor or Tyre. Ramses II himself, the Sesostris of the Greeks, battled for long years against the Hittites on the plains of Canaan, and established a line of Egyptian fortresses as far north as Damascus. The tablets which he engraved at the mouth of the Dog River, near Beyrût, still remain to testify to his victories and campaigns. Representations were sculptured on the walls of Thebes of the forts of "Tabor, in the land of the Amorites," of Merom and of Salem ; and the capture of the revolted city of Ashkelon was celebrated both in sculpture and in song.

But the most interesting record which has come down to us from his reign is the account given by a *mohar*, or military officer, of his travels through Palestine, at a time when the country was nominally tributary to Egypt. The *mohar* made his tour during the latter part of the reign of Ramses II, the oppressor of the Israelites, so that the account he has given of Canaan shows us what it was like shortly before its conquest by Joshua. He journeyed

[1] Called Anab, "(the city of) grapes," in Josh. xi. 21.

as far north as Aleppo in a chariot, which is more than a
traveller in Palestine could do now, and describes how
his clothes were stolen one night, and how his own
groom, or "muleteer," joined the robbers. Among the
places he visited were the Phœnician cities of Gebal,
famous for its shrine of Ashtoreth, Beyrût, Sarepta, Sidon,
and Tyre, which he says was built on an island in the
sea, drinking-water being conveyed to it in boats. Old
Tyre, on the continent opposite, seems to have been
recently burnt. Hamath, Timnah, Hazor, Tabor,
Horonaim, and perhaps Adullam, were also visited, and
mention is made not only of the ford of the Jordan, near
Beth-Shean, but also of "a passage" in front of the city
of Megiddo, which had to be crossed before the town
could be entered. Joppa, the modern Jaffa, was surrounded with gardens of date-palms, which have now
been supplanted by oranges. The road, however, was
not always good. In one place the *mohar* had to
"drive along the edge of the precipice, on the slippery
height, over a depth of 2,000 cubits, full of rocks and
boulders;" while at another time his groom broke the
chariot in pieces by driving over a slippery path, and
necessitated the repair of the injured carriage by "the
iron-workers" at the nearest smithy. Already, therefore, it is clear, Palestine possessed plenty of smithies at
which iron was forged.

That Ramses II was the Pharaoh of the oppression,
has long been suspected by Egyptian scholars. The
accounts of the wars of himself and his predecessors in
Canaan show that up to the date of his death that
country was not yet inhabited by the Israelites. Not
only is no mention made of them, but the history of the
Book of Judges precludes our supposing that Palestine

could have been an Egyptian province after the Israelitish conquest. It must have ceased to be tributary to the Pharaohs before it was entered by Joshua. Moreover, the name of the city of Ramses (Raamses) built by the Israelites in Egypt points unmis-takeably to the reign of the great Ramses II himself. As has already been observed, the name was given to Zoan after its reconstruction by this monarch, whose grandfather, Ramses I, was the first Egyptian king who bore the name. As Ramses I reigned but a very few years, while his successor, Seti I, associated his son, Ramses II, with him on the throne when the latter was but twelve years old or thereabouts, it could only have been during his long reign of sixty-seven years that Ramses II brought the name by which he had been christened into vogue. It is possible that those Egyptian scholars are right who see the Hebrews in a certain class of foreigners called Aperiu, and employed by Ramses II to work at his monuments; if so, we should have another proof that the Exodus could not have taken place until after his death. The identification, however, is rendered very doubtful by the fact, that long after the time of Ramses II, a document of the reign of Ramses III speaks of 2,083 Aperiu as settlers in Heliopolis, and describes them as "knights, sons of the kings, and noble lords of the Aperiu, settled people, who dwell in this place." If, therefore, the Aperiu were really the Hebrews, we should have to suppose that some of them who had obtained offices of honour and influence in Egypt remained behind in Heliopolis, the city of Joseph's wife, when their poorer and oppressed kinsmen followed Moses and Aaron into the desert in search of the Promised Land.

However this may be, the question as to the date of
the Exodus, and consequently as to the Pharaoh of the
oppression, has now been finally set at rest by the excavations recently undertaken at Tel el-Maskhûta.   Tel
el-Maskhûta is the name of some large mounds near
Tel el-Kebîr and other places which were the scene of
the late war; and M. Naville, who has excavated them
for the Egyptian Exploration Fund, has found inscriptions in them which show not only that they represent
an ancient city whose religious name was Pithom, while
its civil name was Succoth, but also that the founder of
the city was Ramses II.   In Greek times the city was
called Heroöpolis, or Ero, from the Egyptian word *ara*,
" a store-house," reminding us that Pithom and Raamses,
which the Israelites built for the Pharaoh, were
"treasure-cities" (Exod. i. 11).   M. Naville has even
discovered the treasure-chambers themselves.   They
are very strongly constructed, and divided by brick
partitions from eight to ten feet thick, the bricks being
sun-baked, and made some with and some without
straw.   In these strawless bricks we may see the work
of the oppressed people when the order came : "Thus
saith the Pharaoh, I will not give you straw."

The treasure-chambers occupy almost the whole area
of the old city, the walls of which are about 650 feet
square and 22 feet thick.   Its name Pithom—in
Egyptian Pa-Tum—signifies the city of the Setting
Sun ; and since it had another name, Succoth, we can
now understand how it was that the Israelites started
on their march not from Goshen, but from Succoth
(Ex. xiii. 20), that is, from the very place where they
had been working.   Etham, their next stage, seems to
be the Egyptian fortress of Khetam, while Pi-hahiroth

(Ex. xiv. 2), is probably Pi-keheret, which is mentioned in an inscription found at Tel el-Maskhûta as somewhere in the neighbourhood of the canal that led from the Nile to the Red Sea.

The Pharaoh under whom the Exodus actually took place could not have been Ramses II himself, but his son and successor, Meneptah II, who ascended the throne about B.C. 1325. His reign lasted but a short time, and it was disturbed not only by the flight of the Children of Israel, but also by a great invasion of Northern Egypt by the Libyans, which was with difficulty repulsed. This took place in his fifth year. Three years later a report was sent to him by one of his officials stating that "the passage of tribes of the Shasu (or Beduins) from the land of Edom had been effected through the fortress of Khetam, which is situated in Succoth (Thuku), to the lakes of the city of Pithom, which are in the land of Succoth, in order that they might feed themselves and their herds on the possessions of the Pharaoh." The lakes of Pithom must be those of Bâlah and Timsah, on which Ismailia now stands, not far from Tel el-Maskhûta, and Khetam is the Etham of Scripture. It is possible that Timsah, "the lake of crocodiles," is the *yâm sûph*, or "sea of papyrus reeds," of Scripture, which the translators of the Septuagint erroneously identified with the Red Sea.

Among the incidents connected with the deliverance of the Israelites are two which especially deserve notice. When God appointed Moses to his mission of leading his enslaved brethren out of Egypt, He at the same time revealed Himself by the name of "Jehovah," the special name by which He was henceforth to be known to the Children of Israel. It is unfortunate that

this sacred name has descended to the readers of the
Authorised Version of the Old Testament in a corrupt
and barbarous form. The Hebrew alphabet was designed to express consonants only, not vowels ; these
were supplied by the reader from his knowledge of the
language and its pronunciation. As long as Hebrew
was still spoken, there was little difficulty in doing this ;
but the case was changed when it ceased to be a living
language. A traditional pronunciation of the sacred
records was preserved in the synagogues ; but it necessarily differed in many respects from the pronunciation
which had actually been once in use, and was itself
in danger of being forgotten or altered. To avoid
such a danger, therefore, the so-called Masoretes, or
Jewish scribes, in the sixth century after the Christian
era, invented a system of symbols which should represent the pronunciation of the Hebrew of the Old Testament as read, or rather chanted, at the time in the great
synagogue of Tiberias in Palestine.[1] It is in accordance
with this Masoretic mode of pronunciation that Hebrew
is now taught. But there was one word which the Masoretes of Tiberias either could not or would not pro-
nounce. This was the national name of the God of
Israel. Though used so freely in the Old Testament, it
had come to be regarded with superstitious reverence
before the time when the Greek translation of the
Septuagint was made, and in this translation, accordingly, the word *Kyrios*, "Lord," is substituted for it
wherever it occurs. The New Testament writers natu-

---

[1] The invention of the existing Masoretic system of vowel-points and
accents is ascribed to Mokha of Tiberias (A. D. 570) and his son Moses,
who are said to have based it on a system invented shortly before by Akha
the Babylonian. Only a very few MSS. are known written in the Babylonian system of punctuation.

rally followed the custom of the Septuagint and of their age, and so also did the Masoretes of Tiberias. Wherever the holy name was met with, they read in place of it *Adônai*, "Lord," and hence, when supplying vowel-symbols to the text of the Old Testament they wrote the vowels of *Adônai* under the four consonants, Y H V H, which composed it. This simply meant that *Adônai* was to be read wherever the sacred name was found. In ignorance of this fact, however, the scholars who first revived the study of Hebrew in modern Europe imagined that the vowels of *Adônai* (*ă* or *ĕ*, *o*, and *â*) were intended to be read along with the consonants below which they stood. The result was the hybrid monster *Yĕhovâh*. In passing into England the word became even more deformed. In German the sound of *y* is denoted by the symbol *j*, and the German symbol, but with the utterly different English pronunciation attached to it, found its way into the English translations of the Old Testament Scriptures.

There are two opinions as to what was the actual pronunciation of the sacred name while Hebrew was still a spoken language. On the one hand, we may gather from the contemporary Assyrian monuments that it was pronounced *Yahu*. Wherever an Israelitish name is met with in the cuneiform inscriptions which, like Jehu or Hezekiah, is compounded with the divine title, the latter appears as *Yahu*, Jehu being *Yahua*, and Hezekiah *Khazaki-yahu*. Even according to the Masoretes it must be read *Yeho* (that is, *Yâhu*) when it forms part of a proper name. The early Gnostics, moreover, when they transcribed it in Greek characters, wrote *Iaô*, that is, *Yahô*. On the other hand, the four consonants, Y II V H, can hardly have been pronounced otherwise

E

than as *Yahveh*, and this pronunciation is supported by the two Greek writers Theodoret and Epiphanios, who say that the word was sounded *Yavé*. The form *Yahveh*, however, is incompatible with the form *Yahu* (*Yeho*), which appears in proper names; and it has been maintained that it is due to one of those plays on words, of which there are so many examples in the Old Testament. The spelling with a final *h* was adopted, it has been supposed, in order to remind the reader of the Hebrew verb which signifies "to be," and to which there seems to be a distinct allusion in Exod. iii. 14.[1]

We must now turn to a second incident which is specially connected with the deliverance out of Egypt. This is the rite of circumcision, which was observed in so solemn a manner at the moment when the Israelites had at last crossed the Jordan and were preparing to attack the Canaanites. It was a rite which had been practised by the Egyptians from the most remote times, and had been communicated by them, according to Herodotus, to the Ethiopians. Josephus tells us that the rite was also practised by the Arabs, to whom Herodotus adds the Syrians of Phœnicia, as well as the Kolkhians and the Hittites of Kappadokia. A similar rite is found at the present day among many barbarous tribes in different parts of the world, and distinguishes not only the Jew but the Mohammedan as well.

The name of Moses seems to be of Egyptian derivation. It would correspond to the Egyptian *mes* or *mesu*, "son," which is borne by more than one Egyptian prince

---

[1] A coin from Gaza, of the fourth century B.C., is now in the British Museum, on one side of which is the figure of the Canaanitish Baal in a chariot of fire, but otherwise with the attributes of the Greek Zeus, and with the word YHU (*i.e.*, Yahu or Yeho) written above him in old Phœnician letters.

at the period of the Exodus, and forms part of the name of Ramses, or Ra-mesu, "the son of the sun." The Hebrew spelling of the word with a final *h* is designed to recall the Hebrew *mashâh*, "to draw out" or "deliver," just as the spelling of the Septuagint, Môysês, was influenced by the etymology given by Josephus, which made it a compound of the Egyptian *mô*, "water," and *ysês*, "to rescue from a flood." Such plays upon words are common in ancient literature, and are still in favour in the East, and we must be on our guard against ascribing to them a scientific value which they do not possess. The name *mesu*, "son," would be an appropriate one for a child who had been adopted by an Egyptian lady, and who was brought up at the court of the Pharaoh in "all the wisdom of the Egyptians."

This chapter would be incomplete unless something were said of the illustrations of the law and ritual of the Israelites afforded by the monuments of the nations around them. These illustrations are to be found among the Phœnicians and the Assyrians. Among both we find traces of sacrifices and institutions which offer many parallels to the ordinances of the Mosaic Law. Besides the Sabbaths already spoken of, the Babylonians and Assyrians had various festivals and fasts, on which certain rites had to be performed and certain sacrifices offered ; they knew of "peace-offerings" and of "heave-offerings," of the dedication of the first-born, and of sacrifices for sin. The gods were carried in procession in "ships," which, as we learn from the sculptures, resembled in form the Hebrew ark, and were borne on men's shoulders by means of staves. In front of the image of the god stood a table, on which showbread was laid ; and a distinction was drawn between the meal-offering and the animal sacrifice. Certain unclean kinds of food were forbidden, including the flesh of swine and "creeping things;" and in the outer courts of the temples were large lavers called "seas," like the "sea" of Solomon's temple, in which the worshippers were required to cleanse themselves. Many of these regulations and rites came down from the Accadian period.

As a specimen of the rites which had to be performed, we may quote a portion of a tablet which prescribes the duties of the priest in the great temple of Bel at Babylon. The tablet begins: "In the month Nisan, on the 2nd day, two hours after nightfall, the priest must come and take of the waters of the river, must enter into the presence of Bel, and change his dress, must put on a . . . robe in the presence of Bel, and say this prayer: 'O my lord, who in his strength has no equal, O my lord, blessed sovereign, lord of the world, speeding the peace of the great gods, the lord who in his might destroys the strong, lord of kings, light of mankind, establisher of trust, O Bel, thy sceptre is Babylon, thy crown is Borsippa, the wide heaven is the dwelling-place of thy liver . . . . O lord of the world, light of the spirits of heaven, utterer of blessings, who is there whose mouth murmurs not of thy righteousness, or speaks not of thy glory, and celebrates not thy dominion? O lord of the world, who dwellest in the temple of the sun, reject not the hands that are raised to thee, be merciful to thy city Babylon, to Beth-Saggil thy temple, incline thy face, grant the prayers of thy people the sons of Babylon.'"

Our knowledge of the Phœnician ritual is largely derived from a sacrificial tariff discovered at Marseilles in 1845. The stone on which it is engraved is unfortunately not perfect, but what is left of it runs thus: "In the temple of Baal (the following tariff of offerings shall be observed), which was prescribed (in the time of) the judge . . . . Baal, the son of Bod-Tanit, the son of Bod-(Ashmun, and in the time of Halzi-Baal), the judge, the son of Bod-Ashmun, the son of Halzi-Baal and (their comrades). For an ox as a full-offering, whether it be a prayer-offering or a full thank-offering, the priests (shall receive) ten shekels of silver for each beast, and if it be a full-offering the priests shall receive besides this (300 shekels' weight of flesh). And for a prayer-offering they shall receive (besides) the small joints (?) and the roast (?), but the skin and the haunches and the feet and the rest of the flesh shall belong to the offerer. For a bullock which has horns, but is not yet broken in and made to serve, or for a stag, as a full-offering, whether it be a prayer-offering or a full thank-offering, the priests (shall receive) five shekels of silver (for each beast, and if it be a full-offering) they shall receive besides this 150 shekels' weight of flesh ; and for a prayer-offering the small joints (?) and the roast (?) ; but the skin and the haunches and the feet (and the rest of the flesh shall belong to the offerer). For a sheep or a goat as a full-offering, whether it be a prayer-offering or a full thank-offering, the priests (shall receive) one shekel of silver and two *zar* for each beast ; and in the case of a prayer-offering they shall have (besides this the small joints [?]) and the roast (?) ; but the skin and the haunches and the feet and the rest of the flesh shall belong to the offerer. For a lamb or a kid or a fawn as a full-offering, whether it be a prayer-offering or a full thank-offering, the priests (shall receive) three-fourths of a shekel of silver and (two) *zar* (for each beast ; and in the case of a prayer-offering they shall have) besides this the small joints (?) and the roast (?) ; but the skin and the haunches and the feet and the rest of the flesh shall belong to (the offerer). For a bird, whether wild or tame, as a full-offering, whether it be *shetseph* or *khazuth*, the priests (shall receive) three-fourths of a shekel of silver and two *zar* for each bird ; and (so much flesh besides). For a bird, or for the offering of the first-born of an animal, or for a meal-offering or for an offering with oil, the priests (shall receive) ten pieces of gold for each . . . . In the case of every prayer-offering which is offered to the gods, the priests shall receive the small joints (?), and the roast (?) and the prayer-offering . . . . for a cake and for milk and for fat, and for every offering which is offered without blood . . . . For every offering which is brought by a poor man in cattle or birds, the priests shall receive nothing . . . . anything leprous or scabby or lean is forbidden, and no one as regards that which he offers (shall taste of) the blood of the dead. The tariff for each offering shall be according to that which is prescribed in this publication . . . . As for every offering which is not prescribed in this table, and is not made according to the regulations which (have been published in the time of . . . . Baal, the son of Bod-Tanit), and of Bod-Ashmun, the son of Halzi-Baal, and of their comrades, every priest who accepts the offering which is not included in that which is prescribed in this table, shall be punished . . . . As for the property of the offerer who does not discharge (his debt) for his offering (he also shall be punished ").

The words that are wanting in the document have been partially supplied from the fragments of another copy of the tariff found among the ruins of Carthage. It will be observed that there is no mention in it of the sacrifice of children, which, as we know, once played a large part in the ritual of the Phœnicians. This is explained by the fact that the tariff belongs to that later age, when Greek and Roman influence had prevailed upon the Phœnician colonists in the west to give up the horrible practice. The place of the child is taken by the *'ayyâl* or stag.

The tariff of Marseilles and Carthage has lately been supplemented by some Phœnician texts found in the island of Cyprus, and written in black and red ink upon small pieces of marble. One of these has both faces inscribed, and a translation of its contents is worth giving. On the first face we read: "Expenses of the month Ethanim: On the new-moon of the month Ethanim, for the gods of the new-moon two . . . . For the architects who have built the temples of Ashtoreth, for each house . . . . For the guardians of the sanctuary and the overseers of the temple of Resheph 20 . . . . For the men (who tend) the cattle in the presence of the Holy Queen on this day . . . . For two boys two . . . For two sacrifices . . . For two bakers who have baked the cakes for the (Holy) Queen . . . . For the barbers, for their work, two . . . . For the ten masons who have built the foundations and the temples of the Sun-god . . . To Ebed-Ashmun, the principal scribe, who has been sent on this day, three . . . . For the dogs and their young . . . ." On the other face we have: "On the new-moon of the month Peûlat: For the gods of the new-moon two . . . . For the masters of the days, incense and peace-offering . . . . For the images of the temple of the Sun-god and the other gods . . . .

For Ebed-Bast of Carthage . . . . For the man who has bought the withered plants (?) . . . . For the shepherds of the country two . . . . For the *'almâth* and the 22 *'alâmôth*, with a sacrifice . . . . For the dogs and their young three . . . ."

Here we evidently have an account of the payments disbursed by the priests of a temple on particular days. Resheph was a title of the Sun-god, and M. Clermont-Ganneau has pointed out that his name still survives in that of Arsûf, a ruined town to the north of Jaffa. The cakes baked for Ashtoreth, "the Holy Queen," are the same as those which the Jewish men and women who had fled to Egypt after the destruction of Jerusalem and the murder of Gedaliah declared to Jeremiah that they would still continue to offer to "the queen of heaven" (Jer. xliv. 19). What is meant by the "dogs" is best explained by Deuteronomy xxiii. 18, while the barbers mentioned in the text were required to shave the priests. Mention is also made of them in the Assyrian inscriptions (see Lev. xix. 27, xxi. 5). The *'almâth*, or "maiden"—a word which has acquired a special significance in the Christian Church in consequence of its having been used in Isaiah's prophecy of "the Virgin" (Isa. vii. 14)—here seems to mean the chief singer attached to the temple of Ashtoreth. The *'alâmôth* are described in the sixty-eighth Psalm (ver. 25) as similarly employed in the worship of Israel. As for the "Masters of the Days," they are the gods who, as among the Assyrians, were believed to preside over the months of the year. The month Ethanim, to which the first account refers, is mentioned, it will be remembered, in 1 Kings viii. 2, as being the month in which the feast of the dedication of Solomon's temple was held. That

temple had been built with the help of Phœnician
workmen, and it was therefore natural that the names of
the Phœnician months should have become known to the
Israelites in connection with it. The Israelites themselves were still contented to speak of the months of the
year according to the order in which they came. It
was not until after the return from the Babylonish exile
that special names for the months were definitely
adopted, and that the Jews henceforth called them by
the Assyrian names they had heard in Babylonia.
What these names were will be found given in full in
the second Appendix.

CHAPTER IV.

The Moabite Stone and the Inscription of Siloam.

*The alphabet of Egyptian origin.—Discovery of the Moabite Stone.—Trans-
lation of the inscription.—Points of interest raised by the inscription.—
Discovery of the Siloam inscription.—The translation.—The date.—Its
bearing upon the topography of Jerusalem.*

MODERN discovery has as yet thrown little contemporary light on the period of Israelitish history which
extends from the conquest of Canaan to the time when
the kingdom of David was rent into the two monarchies
of Israel and Judah. The buried ruins of Phœnicia
have not yet been explored, and we have still to depend
on the statements of classical writers for what we know.
outside the Bible records, of Hiram the Tyrian king, the
friend of David and Solomon. It is certain, however,
that state archives already existed in the chief cities of
Phœnicia, and a library was probably attached to the
ancient temple of Baal, the Sun-god, at Tyre, which was
restored by Hiram. It was from the Phœnicians that
the Israelites, and the nations round about them, received
their alphabet. This alphabet was of Egyptian origin.
As far back as the monuments of Egypt carry us, we
find the Egyptians using their hieroglyphics to express
not only ideas and syllables, but also the letters of an
alphabet. Even in the remote epoch of the second
dynasty they already possessed an alphabet in which the
twenty-one simple sounds of the language were represented by special hieroglyphic pictures. Such hiero-

glyphic pictures, however, were employed only on the public monuments; for books and letters and business transactions the Egyptians made use of a running hand, in which the original pictures had undergone great transformations. This running hand is termed "hieratic," and it was from the hieratic forms of the Egyptian letters that the Phœnician letters were derived.

We have already seen that the coast of the Delta was so thickly peopled with Phœnician settlers as to have acquired the name of Keft-ur, or Caphtor, "greater Phœnicia;" and these settlers it must have been who first borrowed the alphabet of their Egyptian neighbours. For purposes of trade they must have needed some kind of writing, by means of which they could communicate with the natives of the country, and their business-like instincts led them to adopt only the alphabet used by the latter, and to discard all the cumbrous machinery of ideographs and syllabic characters by which it was accompanied. It was doubtless in the time of the Hyksos that the Egyptian alphabet became Phœnician. From the Delta it was handed on to the mother country of Phœnicia, and there the letters received new names, derived from objects to which they bore a resemblance and which began with the sounds they represented. These names, as well as the characters to which they belonged, have descended to ourselves, for the Phœnician alphabet passed first from the Phœnicians to the Greeks, then from the Greeks to the Romans, and finally from the Romans to the nations of modern Europe. The very word *alphabet* is a living memorial of the fact, since it is composed of *alpha* and *beta*, the Greek names of the two first letters, and these names are simply the Phœnician *aleph*, "an ox," and *beth*, "a house." Just as in our own nursery days it was imagined that we should remember our lessons better if we were taught that "A was an Archer who shot at a frog," so the forms of the letters were impressed on the memory of the Phœnician boys by being likened to the head of an ox or the outline of a house.

But before the alphabet was communicated to Greece by the Phœnician traders, it had already been adopted by their Semitic kinsmen in Western Asia. Excavations in Palestine and the country east of the Jordan would doubtless bring to light inscriptions compiled in it much older than the oldest which we at present know. Only a few years ago the gap between the time when the Phœnicians first borrowed their new alphabet and the time to which the earliest texts written in it belonged was very great indeed. But during the last fifteen years two discoveries have been made which help to fill it up, and prove to us at the same time what may be found if we will only seek.

One of these discoveries is that of the famous Moabite Stone. In the summer of 1869, Dr. Klein, a German missionary, while travelling in what was once the land of Moab, discovered a most curious relic of antiquity among the ruins of Dhibân, the ancient Dibon. This relic was a stone of black basalt, rounded at the top, two feet broad and nearly four feet high. Across it ran an inscription of thirty-four lines in the letters of the Phœnician alphabet. Dr. Klein unfortunately did not realise the importance of the discovery he had made ; he contented himself with copying a few words, and endeavouring to secure the monument for the Berlin Museum. Things always move slowly in the East, and it was not until a year later that the negociations for the purchase

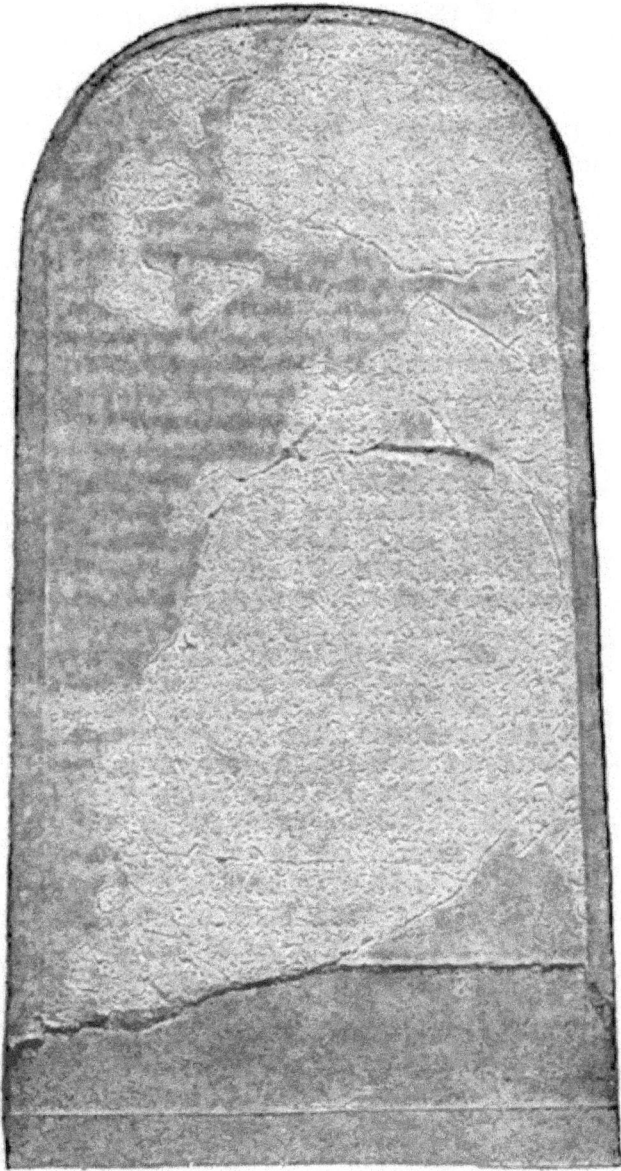

The Moabite Stone, erected by King Mesha, at Dibon.

of the stone were completed between the Prussian Government on the one side and the Arabs and Turkish pashas on the other. At length, however, all was arranged, and it was agreed that the stone should be handed over to the Germans for the sum of £80. At this moment M. Clermont-Ganneau, a member of the French Consulate at Jerusalem, with lamentable indiscretion, sent men to take squeezes of the inscription, and offered no less than £375 for the stone itself. At once the cupidity of both Arabs and pashas was aroused; the Governor of Nablûs demanded the treasure for himself, while the Arabs, fearing it might be taken from them, put a fire under it, poured cold water over it, broke it in pieces, and distributed the fragments as charms among the different families of the tribe. Thanks to M. Clermont-Ganneau, most of these fragments have now been recovered, and the stone, once more put together, may be seen in the Museum of the Louvre at Paris. The fragments have been fitted into their proper places by the help of the imperfect squeezes taken before the monument was broken.

When the inscription came to be read, it turned out to be a record of Mesha, king of Moab, of whom we are told in 2 Kings iii. that after Ahab's death he "rebelled against the king of Israel," and was vainly besieged in his capital Kirharaseth by the combined armies of Israel, Judah and Edom. Mesha describes the successful issue of his revolt, and the revenge he took upon the Israelites for their former oppression of his country. The translation of the inscription is as follows:—

"I, Mesha, am the son of Chemosh-Gad, king of Moab, the Dibonite. My father reigned over Moab thirty years, and I reigned after my father. And I erected this stone to Chemosh at Kirkha, a (stone of) salvation, for he saved me from all despoilers, and made me see my desire upon all my enemies, even upon Omri, king of Israel. Now they afflicted Moab many days, for Chemosh was angry with his land. His son succeeded him; and he also said, I will afflict Moab. In my days (Chemosh) said, (Let us go) and I will see my desire on him and his house, and I will destroy Israel with an everlasting destruction. Now Omri took the land of Medeba, and (the enemy) occupied it in (his days and in) the days of his son, forty years. And Chemosh (had mercy) on it in my days; and I fortified Baal-Meon, and made therein the tank, and I fortified Kiriathaim. For the men of Gad dwelt in the land of (Atar)oth from of old, and the king (of) Israel fortified for himself Ataroth, and I assaulted the wall and captured it, and killed all the warriors of the wall for the well-pleasing of Chemosh and Moab; and I removed from it all the spoil, and (offered) it before Chemosh in Kirjath; and I placed therein the men of Siran and the men of Mochrath. And Chemosh said to me, Go take Nebo against Israel. (And I) went in the night, and I fought against it from the break of dawn till noon, and I took it and slew in all seven thousand (men, but I did not kill) the women (and) maidens, for (I) devoted them to Ashtar-Chemosh; and I took from it the vessels of Yahveh, and offered them before Chemosh. And the king of Israel fortified Jahaz and occupied it, when he made war against me; and Chemosh drove him out before (me, and) I took from Moab two hundred men, all its poor, and placed them in Jahaz, and took it to annex it to Dibon. I built Kirkha, the wall of the forest, and the wall of the city, and I built the gates thereof, and I built the towers thereof, and I built the palace, and I made the prisons for the criminals within the walls. And there was no cistern in the wall at Kirkha, and I said to all the people, Make for yourselves, every man, a cistern in his house. And I dug the ditch for Kirkha by means of the (captive) men of Israel. I built Aroer, and I made the road across the Arnon. I built Beth-Bamoth, for it was destroyed; I built Bezer, for it was cut (down) by the armed men of Dibon, for all Dibon was now loyal; and I reigned from Bikran, which I added to my land, and I built (Beth-Gamul) and Beth-Diblathaim and Beth-Baal-Meon, and I placed there the poor (people) of the land. And as to Horonaim, (the men of Edom) dwelt therein (from of old). And Chemosh said to me, Go down, make war against Horonaim and take (it. And I assaulted it, and I took it, and) Chemosh (restored it) in my days. Wherefore I made . . . . year . . . . and I . . . ."

The last line or two, describing the war against the Edomites, is unfortunately lost beyond recovery. The rest of the text, however, it will be seen, is pretty perfect, and is full of interest to Biblical students. The whole inscription reads like a chapter from one of the historical books of the Old Testament. Not only are the phrases the same, but the words and grammatical forms are, with one or two exceptions, all found in Scriptural Hebrew. We learn that the language of Moab differed less from that of the Israelites than does one English dialect from another. Perhaps the most interesting fact disclosed by the inscription is that Chemosh, the national god of the Moabites, had come to be regarded not only as the supreme deity, but even as almost the only object of their worship. Except in the passage which alludes to the dedication of women and maidens to Ashtar-Chemosh, Mesha speaks as a monotheist, and even here the female Ashtar or Ashtoreth is identified with the supreme male deity Chemosh. Like the Assyrian kings, moreover, who ascribed their victories and campaigns to the inspiration of the god Assur, Mesha ascribes his successes to the orders of Chemosh. He uses, in fact, the language of Scripture; as the Lord said to David, "Go and smite the Philistines" (1 Sam. xxiii. 2), so Chemosh is made to say to Mesha, "Go, take Nebo;" and as God promised to "drive out" the Canaanites before Israel, so Mesha declares that Chemosh drove out Israel before him from Jahaz. Mesha even sets up a stone of salvation to Chemosh, like Eben-ezer, "the stone of help," set up by Samuel (1 Sam. vii. 12); and the statement that Chemosh had been "angry with his land," but had made Mesha "see his desire upon all his enemies," reminds us of the well-known passages in which the Psalmist declares that "God shall let me see my desire upon mine oppressors," and the author of the Book of Judges recounts how that "the anger of the Lord was hot against Israel."

The covenant name of the God of Israel itself occurs in the inscription, spelt in exactly the same way as in the Old Testament. Its occurrence is a proof, if any were needed, that the superstition which afterwards prevented the Jews from pronouncing it did not as yet exist. The name under which God was worshipped in Israel was familiar to the nations round about. Nay, more; we gather that even after the attempt of Jezebel to introduce the Baalim of Sidon into the northern kingdom, Yahveh was still regarded as the national god, and that the worship carried on at the high places, idolatrous and contrary as it was to the law, was nevertheless performed in His name. The high-place of Nebo, like so many of the other localities mentioned in the inscription, is also mentioned in the prophecy against Moab contained in Isa. xv. xvi. It is even possible that the words of the verse in the Book of Isaiah in which it is named have undergone transposition, and that the true reading is, " He is gone up to Dibon and to Beth-Bamoth to weep ; Moab shall howl over Nebo and over Medeba." The inscription informs us that Beth-Bamoth, "the house of the high-places," was the name of a place near Dibon, the name of which appears in the last verse of Isaiah xv. under the form of Dimon, the letter *b* being changed by the prophet into *m*, in order to connect it with the word *dâm*, "blood." Kirkha, "the wall of the forest," the modern Kerak, is called Kir of Moab and Kir-haresh or Kir-hareseth by Isaiah, and Kir-heres by Jeremiah, which by a slight change of vocalisation would signify "the wall of the forest." The form Kir-haraseth is also used in the Book of Kings.

The story told by the Stone, and the account of the war against Moab given in the Bible, supplement one another. Dr. Ginsburg has suggested that the deliverance of Moab from Israel was brought about during the reign of Ahaziah, the successor of Ahab, and that Joram, the successor of Ahaziah, was subsequently driven out of Jahaz, which lay on the southern side of the Arnon ; but that after this the tide of fortune turned, Joram summoned his allies from Judah and Edom, ravaged Moab, and block, aded Mesha in his capital of Kirkha. Then came the sacrifice by Mesha of his eldest son on the wall of Kirkha- so that " there was great indignation against Israel," and the allied forces retreated back "to their own land."

F

The Moabite Stone shows us what were the forms of the Phœnician letters used on the eastern side of the Jordan in the time of Ahab. The forms employed in Israel and Judah on the western side could not have differed much; and we may therefore see in these venerable characters the precise mode of writing employed by the earlier prophets of the Old Testament. This knowledge is of great importance for the correction and restoration of corrupt passages, and more especially of proper names, the spelling of which has been deformed by copyists.

Just, however, as the writing of two persons at the present day must differ, so also the writing of two nations like the Moabites and Jews must have differed to some extent. Moreover, there must have been some distinction between the more cursive writing of a papyrus-roll and the carefully cut letters of a public monument like that of Mesha. Indeed, that such a distinction did exist we have proof in a passage (Isa. viii. 1) which has been mistranslated in the Authorised Version, but which ought to be rendered: "Take thee a great slab, and write upon it with the graving-tool of the people: Hasten spoil, hurry booty." Here words which were afterwards to be made more emphatic by becoming the name of one of Isaiah's children, were written in a way that all could read, not in the running hand of a scroll, but in the large clear characters of a public document. What these characters exactly were, a recent discovery has enabled us to learn.

Hebrew inscriptions of an early date have long been sought for in vain. We knew of one or two inscribed fragments from the neighbourhood of the Pool of Siloam at Jerusalem, and of a few seals which might be referred to the period before the Babylonish Captivity ; but, unfortunately, none of these could be assigned to a definite date, and even the conclusion that some of them were pre-exilic was after all little more than a guess. The seals are usually distinguished by the absence of any symbols or other devices, as well as by a horizontal line drawn across the middle, which divides the inscription into two halves. The proper names also which occur on them are, in the majority of cases, compounded with the sacred name Yahveh. Several of these seals have been found in Babylonia and Mesopotamia, and may therefore be regarded as memorials of the Jewish exile. But the legends they bear are always short, and consist of little else than proper names; and as their date was uncertain, it was impossible to draw any solid inferences from them as to the character of the writing employed in Judah or Israel before the age of Nebuchadnezzar.

It is quite otherwise now. An inscription of some length has been discovered in Jerusalem itself, which is certainly as old as the time of Isaiah, and may be older still. In the summer of 1880, one of the native pupils of Mr. Schick, a German architect long settled in Jerusalem, was playing with some other lads in the so-called Pool of Siloam, and while wading up a channel cut in the rock which leads into the Pool, slipped and fell into the water. On rising to the surface, he noticed what looked like letters on the rock which formed the southern wall of the channel. He told Mr. Schick of what he had seen ; and the latter, on visiting the spot, found that an ancient inscription, concealed for the most part by the water, actually existed there.

The Pool is of comparatively modern construction, but it encloses the remains of a much older reservoir, which, like the modern one, was supplied with water through a tunnel excavated in the rock. This tunnel communicates with the so-called Spring of the Virgin, the only natural spring of water in or near Jerusalem. It rises below the walls of the city, on the western bank of the valley of the Kidron; and the tunnel through which its waters are conveyed is consequently cut through the ridge, that forms the southern part of the Temple Hill. The Pool of Siloam lies on the opposite side of this ridge, at the mouth of the valley called that of the Cheesemakers (Tyropœôn) in the time of Josephus, but which is now filled up with rubbish, and in large part built over. According to Lieutenant Conder's measurements, the length of the tunnel is 1,708 yards; it does not, however, run in a straight line, and towards the centre there are two *culs de sac*, of which the inscription now offers an explanation. At the entrance on the western or Siloam side its height is about sixteen feet; but the roof grows gradually lower, until in one place it is not quite two feet above the floor of the passage.

The inscription occupies the under part of an artificial tablet in the wall of rock, about nineteen feet from where the conduit opens out upon the Pool of Siloam, and on the right-hand side of one who enters it. After lowering the level of the water, Mr. Schick endeavoured to take a copy of it; but as not only the letters of the text, but every flaw in the rock were filled with a deposit of lime left by the water, all he could send to Europe was a collection of unmeaning scrawls. Besides the difficulty of distinguishing the letters, it was also necessary to sit in the mud and water, and to work by the dim light of

The Siloam Inscription (tracing from a squeeze, taken 15th July, 1881, by Lieuts. Conder and Mantell, R.E.).

a candle, as the place where the inscription is engraved is perfectly dark. All this rendered it impossible for anyone not acquainted with Phœnician palæography to make an accurate transcript. The first intelligible copy accordingly was made by Professor Sayce after several hours of careful study ; but this too contained several doubtful characters, the real forms of which could only be determined by the removal of the calcareous matter with which they were coated. In March, 1881, six weeks after Sayce's visit, Dr. Guthe arrived in Jerusalem, and after making a more complete facsimile of the inscription than had previously been possible, removed the deposit of lime by means of an acid, and so revealed the original appearance of the tablet. Letters which had previously been concealed now became visible, and the exact shapes of them all could be observed. First a cast, and then squeezes of the text were taken ; and the scholars of Europe had at last in their hands an exact copy of the old text.

The inscription consists of six lines, but several of the letters composing it have unfortunately been destroyed by the wearing away of the rock. The translation of it is as follows :—

1. "(Behold) the excavation ! Now this is the history of the excavation. While the excavators were still lifting up the pick, each towards his neighbour, and while there were yet three cubits to (excavate, there was heard) the voice of one man calling to his neighbour, for there was an excess in the rock on the right hand (and on the left). And after that on the day of excavating the excavators had struck pick against pick, one against the other, the waters flowed from the spring to the Pool for a distance of 1,200 cubits. And (part)

of a cubit was the height of the rock over the head of the excavators."

The language of the inscription is the purest Biblical Hebrew. There is only one word in it—that rendered "excess"—which is new, and consequently of doubtful signification. We learn from it that the engineering skill of the day was by no means despicable. The conduit was excavated in the same fashion as the Mont Cénis tunnel of our own time, by beginning the work simultaneously at the two ends; and, in spite of its windings, the workmen almost succeeded in meeting in the middle. They approached, indeed, so nearly to one another, that the noise made by the one party in hewing the rock was heard by the other, and the small piece of rock which intervened between them was accordingly pierced. This accounts for the two *culs de sac* now found in the centre of the channel; they represent the extreme points reached by the two bands of excavators before they had discovered that, instead of meeting, they were passing by one another.

It is most unfortunate that the inscription contains no indication of date; but the forms of the letters used in it show that it cannot be very much later in age than the Moabite Stone. Indeed, some of the letters exhibit older forms than those of the Moabite Stone; but this may be explained by the supposition that the scribes of Jerusalem were more conservative, more disposed to retain old forms, than the scribes of king Mesha. The prevalent opinion of scholars is that the tunnel and consequently the inscription in it were executed in the reign of Hezekiah. According to the Chronicler (2 Chr. xxxii. 30), Hezekiah "stopped the upper watercourse of Gihon, and brought it straight down to the west side of the city of David," and we read in 2 Kings xx. 20, that "he made a pool and a conduit, and brought water into the city." The object of the laborious undertaking is very plain. The Virgin's Spring, the only natural source near Jerusalem, lay outside the walls, and in time of war might easily pass into the hands of the enemy. The Jewish kings, therefore, did their best to seal up this spring, which must be the Chronicler's "upper water-course of Gihon," and to bring its waters by subterranean passages inside the city walls. Besides the tunnel which contains the inscription another tunnel has been dis-covered, which also communicates with the Virgin's Spring. But it is tempting to suppose that the most important of these—the tunnel which contains the in-scription—must be the one which Hezekiah made.

The supposition, however, is rendered uncertain by a statement of Isaiah (viii. 6). While Ahaz, the father of Hezekiah, was still reigning, Isaiah uttered a prophecy in which he made allusion to "the waters of Shiloah that go softly." Now this can hardly refer to anything else than the gently flowing stream which still runs through the tunnel of Siloam. In this case the conduit would have been in existence before the time of Hezekiah ; and, since we know of no earlier period when a great engineering work of the kind could have been executed until we go back to the reign of Solomon, it is possible that the inscription may actually be of this ancient date. The inference is supported by the name Shiloah, which probably means "the tunnel," and would have been given to the locality in consequence of the conduit which here pierced the rock. It was not likely that when David and Solomon were fortifying Jerusalem, and employing Phœnician architects upon great public buildings there, they would have allowed the city to depend wholly upon rain cisterns for its water supply. Since the inscription calls the Pool of Siloam simply "the Pool," we may perhaps infer that no other reservoir of the kind was in existence at the time; and yet in the age of Isaiah, as we learn from Isa. xxii. 9, 11, there was not only "a lower pool," in contradistinction to "an upper one," but also "an old pool," in contradistinction to a new one. As Dr. Guthe's excavations have laid bare the remains of four such pools in the neighbourhood of that of Siloam, there is no difficulty in finding places for all these reservoirs. But they could hardly have existed when the Pool of Siloam was still known as simply "the Pool," nor could the name of Shiloah have well been given to the locality if another tunnel, observed by Sir Charles Warren on the eastern side of the Temple Hill, had been already excavated. This second tunnel starts, like the Siloam one, from the Virgin's Spring, and was designed to bring the water of the spring within the walls of the city. A shaft is cut for seventy feet into the hill, where it meets another perpendicular shaft, which rises for a height of fifty feet, and then meets a flight of steps, which lead into a broad passage, ending in another flight of steps and a vaulted chamber. Niches for lamps were found here at intervals, intended to light the persons who went to draw the water by means of a bucket. As lamps of the Roman period were discovered in the chamber, the tunnel must have been known and used up to the time of the capture of Jerusalem by Titus, and it is probably not older than the reign of Herod. In any case, the comparative excellence of its workmanship goes to show that it was made at a later date than the tunnel of Siloam.

Whatever doubts, however, may still hang over the
date of the inscription, there can be no question that
it has thrown most important light on the topography
of Jerusalem in the period of the kings. It is now clear
that the modern city occupies very little of the same
ground as the ancient one ; the latter stood entirely on
the rising ground to the east of the Tyropœôn valley,
the northern portion of which is at present occupied by
the mosque of Omar, while the southern portion is uninhabited. The Tyropœôn valley itself must be the
Valley of the Son of Hinnom, where the idolaters of
Jerusalem burnt their children in the fire to Moloch. It
must be in the southern cliff of this valley that the tombs
of the kings are situated ; the reason why they have
never yet been found being that they are buried under
the rubbish with which the valley is filled. Among the
rubbish must be the remains of the city which was
destroyed by Nebuchadnezzar, and whose ruins were
flung into the gorge below. Between the higher part
of the hill, now occupied by the mosque of Omar, and
its lower uninhabited portion, Dr. Guthe has discovered
traces of a valley which once ran into the valley of the
Kidron at right angles to it, not far from the Virgin's
Spring, and divided in old days the City of David from
the rest of the town. Here, as well as in the now
obliterated Valley of the Cheesemakers, there probably
still lie the relics of the dynasty of David ; but we shall
only know the story they have to tell us when the
spade of the excavator has come to continue the discoveries which the inscription of Siloam has begun.

CHAPTER V.

THE EMPIRE OF THE HITTITES.

Discovery of traces of an ancient Hittite Empire—Scripture references to the Hittites.—Professor Sayce's discovery.—The inscriptions at Hamath.— The Hittite race.—Hittite art.

FIVE years ago there was no one who suspected that a great empire had once existed in Western Asia and contended on equal terms with both Egypt and Assyria, the founders of which were the little-noticed Hittites of the Old Testament. Still less did any one dream that these same Hittites had once carried their arms, their art, and their religion to the shores of the Ægean, and that the early civilisation of Greece and Europe was as much indebted to them as it was to the Phœnicians.

The discovery was made in 1879. Recent exploration and excavation had shown that the primitive art and culture of Greece, as revealed, for example, by Dr. Schliemann's excavations at Mykenæ, were influenced by a peculiar art and culture emanating from Asia Minor. Here, too, certain strange monuments had been discovered, which form a continuous chain from Lydia in the west to Kappadokia and Lykaonia in the east. The best known of these are certain rock sculptures found at Boghaz Keui and Eyuk, on the eastern side of the Halys, and two figures in relief in the Pass of Karabel, near Sardes, which the old Greek historian, Herodotus, had long ago supposed to be memorials of the Egyptian conqueror Sesostris, or Ramses II.

Meanwhile other discoveries were being made in lands more immediately connected with the Bible. Scholars had learned from the Egyptian inscriptions that before the days of the Exodus the Egyptian monarchs had been engaged in fierce struggles with the powerful nation of the Hittites, whose two chief seats were at Kadesh on the Orontes and Carchemish on the Euphrates, and who were able to summon to their aid subject-allies not only from Palestine, but also far away from Lydia and the Troad, on the western coast of Asia Minor. Ramses II himself, the Pharaoh of the oppression, had been glad to make peace with his antagonists ; and the treaty, which provided, among other things, for the amnesty of political offenders who had found a shelter during the war among one or other of the two combatants, was cemented by the marriage of the Egyptian king with the daughter of his rival. A century or two afterwards Tiglath-Pileser I of Assyria found his passage across the Euphrates barred by the Hittites of Carchemish and their Kolkhian mercenaries. From this time forward the Hittites proved dangerous enemies to the Assyrian kings in their attempts to extend the empire towards the west, until at last in B.C. 717 Sargon succeeded in capturing their rich capital, Carchemish, and in making it the seat of an Assyrian satrap. Henceforth the Hittites disappear from history.

But they had already left their mark on the pages of the Old Testament. The Canaanite who had betrayed his fellow-citizens at Beth-el to the Israelites dared not entrust himself to his countrymen, but went away " into the land of the Hittites " (Judges i. 26). Solomon imported horses from Egypt, which he sold to the Syrians and the Hittites (1 Kings x. 28, 29), and when

God had sent a panic upon the camp of the Syrians
before Jerusalem, they had imagined that "the king of
Israel had hired against them the kings of the Hittites
and the kings of the Egyptians" (2 Kings vii. 6).
Kadesh itself, the southern Hittite capital, is mentioned
in a passage where the Hebrew text is unfortunately
corrupt (2 Sam. xxiv. 6). Here the Septuagint shows
us that the officers sent by David to number the people,
in skirting the northern frontier of his kingdom, came as
far as "Gilead and the land of the Hittites of Kadesh."
In the extreme south of Palestine an offshoot of the
race had been settled from an early period. These are
the Hittites of whom we hear in Genesis in connection
with the patriarchs. Hebron was one of their cities,
and Hebron, we are told (Numb. xiii. 22), "was built
seven years before Zoan," or Tanis, the capital of the
Hyksos conquerors of Egypt. This suggests that the
Hittites formed part of the Hyksos forces, and that
some of them, instead of entering Egypt, remained
behind in Southern Canaan. The suggestion is confirmed by a statement of the Egyptian historian
Manetho, who asserts that Jerusalem was founded by
the Hyksos after their expulsion from Egypt; and
Jerusalem, it will be remembered, had, according to
Ezekiel (xvi. 3), a Hittite mother.

Another Hittite city in the south of Judah was
Kirjath-sepher, or "Booktown," also known as Debir,
"the sanctuary," a title which reminds us of that of
Kadesh, "the holy city." We may infer from its name
that Kirjath-sepher contained a library stocked with
Hittite books. That the Hittites were a literary people,
and possessed a system of writing of their own, we learn
from the Egyptian monuments. What this writing was

has been revealed by recent discoveries. Inscriptions in a peculiar kind of hieroglyphics or picture-writing have been found at Hamath, Aleppo, and Carchemish, in Kappadokia, Lykaonia, and Lydia. They are always found associated with sculptures in a curious style of art, some of which from Carchemish, the modern Jerablûs, are now in the British Museum. The style of art is the same as that of the monuments of Asia Minor mentioned above.

It was the discovery of this fact by Professor Sayce, in 1879, which first revealed the existence of the Hittite empire and its importance in the history of civilisation. Certain hieroglyphic inscriptions, originally noticed by the traveller Burckhardt at Hamah, the ancient Hamath, had been made accessible to the scientific world by the Palestine Exploration Fund, and the conjecture had been put forward that they represented the long-lost writing of the Hittites. The conjecture was shortly afterwards confirmed by the discovery of similar inscriptions at Jerablûs, which Mr. Skene and Mr. George Smith had already identified with the site of Carchemish. If, therefore, the early monuments of Asia Minor were really of Hittite origin, as Professor Sayce supposed, it was clear that they ought to be accompanied by Hittite hieroglyphics. And such turned out to be the case. On visiting the sculptured figure in the Pass of Karabel, in which Herodotus had seen an image of the great opponent of the Hittites, he found that the characters engraved by the side of it were all of them Hittite forms.

Hittite inscriptions have since been discovered attached to another archaic monument of Lydia, the sitting figure of the great goddess of Carchemish, carved out of the rocks of Mount Sipylos, which the Greeks fancied was the Niobê of their mythology as far back as the age of Homer; and similar inscriptions also exist at Boghaz Keui and Eyuk, in Kappadokia, as well as near Ivris, in Lykaonia. Others have been discovered in various parts of Kappadokia and in the Taurus range of mountains, while a silver boss, which bears a precious inscription both in Hittite hieroglyphics and in cuneiform characters, seems to belong to Cilicia. In fact, there is now abundant evidence that the Hittites once held dominion throughout the greater portion of Asia Minor, so that we need no longer feel surprised at their being able to call Trojans and Lydians to their aid in their wars against Egypt.

The existence of Hittite inscriptions at Hamath goes to show that Hamath also was once under Hittite rule. This throws light on several facts recorded in sacred history. David, after his conquest of the Syrians, became the ally of the Hamathite king, and the alliance seems to have lasted down to the time when Hamath was finally destroyed by the Assyrians, since it is implied in the words of 2 Kings xiv. 28, as well as in the alliance between Uzziah and Hamath, of which we are informed by the Assyrian monuments. Hamath and Judah, in fact, each had a common enemy in Syria, and were thus drawn together by a common interest. It was only when Assyria threatened all the populations of the west alike, that Hamath and Damascus were found fighting side by side at the battle of Karkar. Otherwise they were natural foes.

The reason of this lay in the fact that the Hittites were intruders in the Semitic territory of Syria. Their origin must be sought in the highlands of Kappadokia, and from hence they descended into the regions of the south, at that time occupied by Semitic Arameans. Hamath and Kadesh had once been Aramean cities, and when they were again wrested from the possession of the Hittites they did but return to their former owners. The fall of Carchemish meant the final triumph of the Semites in their long struggle with the Hittite stranger.

Even in their southern home the Hittites preserved the dress of the cold mountainous country from which they had come. They are characterised by boots with turned-up toes, such as are still worn by the mountaineers of Asia Minor and Greece. They were thick-set and somewhat short of limb, and the Egyptian artists painted them without beards, of a yellowish-white colour, with dark black hair. In short, as M. Lenormant has pointed out, they had all the physical characteristics of a Caucasian tribe. Their descendants are still to be met with in the defiles of the Taurus and on the plateau of Kappadokia, though they have utterly forgotten the language or languages their forefathers spoke. What this language was is still uncertain, though the Hittite proper names which occur on the monuments of Egypt and Assyria show that it was neither Semitic nor Indo-European. With the help of the bilingual inscription in cuneiform and Hittite, already mentioned, Professor Sayce believes that he has determined the values of a few characters and partially read three or four names, but until more inscriptions are brought to light it is impossible to proceed further. Only it is becoming every day more probable that the hieroglyphics in which the inscriptions are written were the origin of a curious syllabary once used throughout Asia Minor, which survived in Cyprus into historical times.

G

Hittite art was originally borrowed from Babylonia, but modified by the borrowers in a peculiar way. The borrowing took place before the rise of Assyria. The astronomical and astrological tablets belonging to the great work on the heavenly bodies which was compiled for the library of Sargon I of Accad speak from time to time of the Khattâ or Hittites, a clear proof that already at that remote epoch they had moved down from their northern home into their new quarters in Syria. Besides the art of Babylonia they also borrowed several of the Babylonian deities and religious legends. The supreme goddess of Carchemish was the Babylonian Istar or Ashtoreth, and the representation of her found on early Babylonian cylinders was carried by the Hittites to the western coasts of Asia Minor, and from thence made its way across the Ægean Sea to Greece. Even the Amazons of Greek mythology were really nothing more than the priestesses of this Hittite divinity, who wore arms in honour of the goddess. The cities which according to the Greeks were founded by the Amazons were all of Hittite origin.

We may expect to discover hereafter that the influence exercised by the Hittites upon their Syrian neighbours was almost as profound as that exercised by them upon their neighbours in Asia Minor, and through these upon the fathers of the Greeks. For the present, however, we must be content with the startling results that have already been obtained in this new field of research. A people that once played an important part in the history of the civilised world has been again revealed to us after centuries of oblivion, and a forgotten empire has been again brought to light. The first chapter has been opened of a new history, which can only be completed when more Hittite inscriptions have been discovered, and the story they contain has been deciphered. All that is now needed are explorers and excavators, who shall do for the buried cities of the Hittites what Botta and Layard have done for Nineveh or Schliemann for Mykenæ and Troy.

CHAPTER VI.

THE ASSYRIAN INVASIONS.

WHEN David founded his empire his two powerful neighbours, Egypt and Assyria, were both in a state of decline. Assyria had fallen into the hands of unwarlike kings, who were unable to retain the conquests of their predecessors, even upon their immediate frontiers ; while Egypt was divided among rival dynasties and rent with civil wars. Egypt, however, was the first to recover her strength. The monarchs of the twenty-second dynasty once more united the country under one rule, and Shishak or Sheshank I turned his arms against the cities of Palestine. The brief account given in 1 Kings xiv. 25, 26, and the fuller history in 2 Chron. xii. of his invasion of Judah and his capture of Jerusalem, are supplemented by his own record of it on the walls of the ruined temple of Karnak. Here the Egyptian king is represented as striking down the conquered Hebrews with a colossal club, while beside him run long rows of embattled shields, within each of which is the name of a vanquished city. Among them we find the names not only of Jewish towns but of Israelitish fortresses also— such as Megiddo, Taanach, and Abel—a proof that the Egyptian campaign was directed against the northern kingdom as well as against Judah, and could not, there- fore, have been undertaken at the instigation of Jero- boam, as has sometimes been supposed. One of the cities is called Judah-melek, or "Judah-king," a title by which it is possible that Jerusalem may have been intended. At any rate, there is otherwise no mention of the royal city of Rehoboam among the shields that have been preserved.

The vigorous rule of Shishak had not ceased long before Egypt once more sank into a state of anarchy and weakness, which ended in its conquest by the Ethiopian Sabako, the So of the Old Testament (2 Kings xvii. 4). Meanwhile Assyria had recovered its strength, and had entered upon a new career of conquest. In B.C. 858 Shalmaneser II came to the throne, and his long reign of thirty-five years was one continuous history of campaigns against his neighbours, in the course of which the authority of Assyria was extended as far as the Mediterranean. The growing power of Damascus, which Rezon had torn from the empire of David in the time of Solomon (1 Kings xi. 23–25), formed the chief object of his attack. Already, in the sixth year of his reign, he had overthrown the combined forces of Damascus, of Hamath, and of the Hittites, and had slain 20,500 of his enemies in battle. Damascus was at this time governed by Hadad-idri or

Hadadezer, the Ben-hadad II of Scripture, the Scriptural name being a standing title of the Syrian kings, and signifying "the son of Hadad," the supreme deity of Damascus. Three years later Shalmaneser again attacked the Syrian king; but it was not until his fourteenth year, when he crossed the Euphrates with an army of 120,000 men, that he achieved any substantial success.

The campaign of the sixth year is narrated in detail in an inscription engraved by the Assyrian monarch on the rocks of Armenia. Here we learn that, after crossing the Euphrates, he received the tribute of the Hittite states in Pethor, the city of Balaam, which he describes as being situated at the junction of the Euphrates and Sajur. He then marched to Aleppo, where more gifts were brought to him, and after capturing three of the fortresses of Hamath, reached the royal city of Karkar or Aroer. This, he says, "I threw down, I dug up, I burned with fire; 1,200 chariots, 1,200 war-magazines, and 20,000 men belonging to Hadadezer of Damascus; 700 chariots, 700 war-magazines, and 10,000 men belonging to Irkhulina of Hamath; 2,000 chariots and 10,000 men belonging to Ahab of Israel (*Sirlâ*); 500 men of the Kuans; 1,000 men from Egypt; 10 chariots and 10,000 men from the land of Irkanat; 2,000 men belonging to Matinu-baal of Arvad; 2,000 men from the land of Usanat; 30 chariots and 10,000 men belonging to Adoni-baal of Sizan; 1,000 men belonging to Gindibuh of the Arabians; and several hundred men belonging to Baasha, the son of Rehob, of the Ammonites—these twelve kings led their troops to its help, and came to make war and fighting against me. By the supreme help which Assur, the lord, gave (me), with the mighty weapons which the great defender who went before me lent (to me), I fought with them. From the city of Karkar, as far as the city of Guzau I overthrew them. Fourteen thousand of their fighting men I slew with weapons; like the Air-god I bade the storm issue forth upon them ; with their corpses I filled the face of the waters ; their vast armies I brought down with my weapons ; there was not room enough in the country for their dead bodies ; to preserve the life of it I brought back a vast multitude, and distributed them among its men. The banks of the River Orontes I reached. In the midst of this battle I took away from them their chariots, their war-magazines, and their horses trained to the yoke."

The first question that presents itself to us when we read this inscription is how we are to reconcile the mention of Ahab in it with the date of the battle of Karkar (B.C. 853). According to the chronology adopted in the margin of our Bibles, Ahab would have been dead long before the event. The Assyrian monuments, however, have proved that this chronology exceeds the true one by more than forty years ; and the date assigned to Ahab by the inscription harmonises completely with the dates that other inscriptions assign to later kings of Israel and Judah. In all probability, the battle of Karkar took place shortly before Ahab's death; and it was no doubt in consequence of the defeat undergone there by the Syrian forces that Ahab was not only enabled to shake off his subjection to Damascus, but also to ally himself with Judah, and endeavour to recover the frontier fortress of Ramoth, of which Israel had been robbed. The alliance between Ahab and the king of Damascus is recorded in 1 Kings xx. 34.

The battle of Karkar must have followed not very long afterwards, since the attack on Ramoth was made within three years after the conclusion of the alliance. Ahab's death may, therefore, be placed in B.C. 851.

Another question that may be asked is how the Assyrian monarch can say that twelve princes were arrayed in arms against him, when, according to his own enumeration, the forces of only eleven nations were present, some of which do not seem to have been under the command of any king. The only answer that can be given is that Shalmaneser is guilty of a similar arithmetical inaccuracy to that which makes him say that 14,000 of the enemy fell in battle, whereas, according to other accounts, the number was really 20,500; though it is possible that the latter number may include the loss in other battles that took place during the campaign besides the decisive one at Karkar. When, however, we find such arithmetical corruptions as these in contemporaneous documents, we need not wonder that the numerical statements of the Old Testament have become changed and uncertain in their passage through the hands of generations of copyists.

We may infer from the fifth chapter of 2 Kings that the god Rimmon was the chief object of worship of Hadadezer or Ben-hadad, the Syrian king. The Assyrian inscriptions have shown us why this was so. Rimmon is the Assyrian Ramman, the Air-god, and Ramman is specially identified with the Syrian deity Hadad, whose name enters into that of Hadadezer. Hadad-Rimmon, in fact, was the supreme divinity of Damascus, where he represented, not the god of the air, as among the Assyrians, but Baal, the Sun-god, himself. Hence it is that in Zechariah xii. 11, reference is made to the "mourning of Hadad-Rimmon in the valley of Megiddo," that is to say, to the yearly festival, when the women mourned for the death of the Sungod, slain, as it was imagined, by the winter. In Phœnicia the god was known as Adônis, the "lord," or under his old Babylonian title of Tammuz. It was for Tammuz, it will be remembered, that Ezekiel saw the women sitting and weeping within the precincts of "the Lord's house" itself in Jerusalem (Ezek. viii. 14).

Hadadezer was murdered between the fourteenth and eighteenth years of Shalmaneser, and the crown seized by Hazael. In his eighteenth year the Assyrian king moved against the usurper, and captured his camp along with 1,121 chariots and 470 war-magazines. The battle took place on the summit of Sanir or Shenir— the name given to Mount Hermon by the Amorites according to Deut. iii. 9—"which lies over against Lebanon." Here 16,000 of the Syrians fell in battle, and Hazael fled to Damascus, whither he was followed by the Assyrians. Damascus, however, proved too strong to be captured, and Shalmaneser accordingly contented himself with cutting down the trees by which it was surrounded, and retiring into the Haurân, where he burnt the unwalled towns, and carried away their inhabitants into captivity. He then followed the high road from Damascus to the Mediterranean, and on the promontory of Baal-rosh, at the mouth of the Dog River, near Beyrût, had an image of himself carved upon the rocks. At the same place he received the tribute of Tyre and Sidon, as well as of "Yahua, the son of Khumri," that is to say, of Jehu, the descendant of Omri. In calling Jehu a descendant of Omri, the Assyrian king was misinformed; he had heard nothing of the revolution which had extirpated the house of Omri, and had placed Jehu upon the throne. Like Ahab, therefore, Jehu was supposed to be a son of Omri, the founder of Samaria, which is frequently termed Beth-Omri, "the house of Omri," in the Assyrian inscriptions, though in the later days of Tiglath-Pileser II and Sargon, "Beth-Omri" is superseded by "Samirina." This was the Aramaic form of the native name Shimrôn, and must consequently have been derived by the Assyrians from the Aramaic neighbours of the Israelites.

In the Assyrian Hall of the British Museum there now stands a small obelisk of black marble, which was brought from Calah by Sir A. H. Layard, on which Shalmaneser records the annals of his reign. The upper portion of the monument is occupied by a series of reliefs representing the tribute brought to the Assyrian monarch by the distant nations which had sought his favour. Among the reliefs is one in which the ambassadors of Jehu are depicted bearing their offerings of gold and silver bars, of a golden vase and a golden spoon, of cups and goblets of gold, of pieces of lead, of a royal sceptre and of clubs of wood. Their features are those which are still characteristic of the Jewish race, and their fringed robes descend to their ankles.

The death of Shalmaneser brought with it a period of peace for Damascus and Palestine. His son and successor turned his arms in other directions, and Hazael and his successor, Ben-hadad III, were left free to ravage Israel (2 Kings xiii. 3). It was not until the Israelites, under Jeroboam II, had taken ample revenge upon the Syrians, and the coast of Israel was restored "from the entering of Hamath unto the sea of the plain," that an

Assyrian monarch once more marched towards the west. This was Rimmon-nirari, grandson of Shalmaneser, who reigned from B.C. 810 to 781, and reduced the kingdom of Damascus to a condition of vassalage. Damascus was now under the government of a king called Marih, the successor, probably, of Ben-hadad III, who, after undergoing a siege at the hands of the Assyrians, was glad to make terms with them by acknowledging the supremacy of Rimmon-nirari, and by giving him 2,300 talents of silver, 20 talents of gold, 3,000 talents of copper, 5,000 talents of iron, embroidered robes and clothes of fine linen, a couch inlaid with ivory and an ivory parasol, besides other treasures and furniture without number which his palace contained. It is very possible that Jeroboam's successes against the Syrians were in large measure due to the extent to which they had been weakened by the Assyrians. Rimmon-nirari also claims to have received tribute from Tyre and Sidon, from Beth-Omri, from Edom, and from Palastu or Palestine—a name under which we should probably include not only the district inhabited by the Philistines, but the kingdom of Judah as well. The tribute was no doubt sent to him after his triumphal entry into Damascus.

With Rimmon-nirari the power of the older dynasty of the Assyrian kings came to an end. His successors were scarcely able to defend themselves against the attacks of their neighbours on the north and south; diseases and insurrections broke out in the great cities of the kingdom, and finally, in B.C. 746, there was a rising in Calah; the king either died or was put to death, and before the year was over, in the month of April, B.C. 745, the crown was seized by a military adventurer, named Pul, who assumed the title of Tiglath-Pileser II. Tiglath-Pileser I had been the most famous monarch and most extensive conqueror of the older dynasty, and had reigned over Assyria five centuries previously; by assuming his name, therefore, the usurper wished to show that he intended to emulate his deeds. According to later tradition, the new king had begun his career as a gardener; whether this were true or not, he showed great military and executive capacities after he had established himself on the throne, and it was to him that the second Assyrian empire owed its origin.

Tiglath-Pileser determined to cement the various states of Western Asia into a single empire, governed by satraps appointed at Nineveh, and accountable only to the king. Each satrapy, or province, had to provide a certain number of men for the imperial army, and to pay a fixed annual tribute to the imperial treasury. Thus, Nineveh itself was assessed at 30 talents, ten of which went to the general expenditure, while the remaining twenty were devoted to the maintenance of the fleet. Calah paid 9 talents; Carchemish, once the rich capital of the Hittites, paid 100; Arpad 30; and Megiddo but 15. Besides gold and silver, the cities and provinces were called upon to furnish chariots, clothing, and other similar contributions.

Two years after his accession (B.C. 743) Tiglath-Pileser II turned his attention to the west. Arpad, now Tel-Erfad, near Aleppo, was the first object of attack. It held out for three years, and did not fall until B.C. 740. But, meanwhile, the kingdom of Hamath had been shattered by the Assyrian arms. Nineteen of its districts were placed under Assyrian governors, and the Assyrian forces made their way as far as the Mediter-

ranean Sea. Azri-yahu, or Azariah (Uzziah), the
Jewish king, had been the ally of Hamath, and from
him also punishment was accordingly exacted.   He was
compelled to purchase peace by the offer of submission and the payment of tribute.   The alliance between
Judah and Hamath had been of long standing.   David
had been the friend of its king Tou or Toi ; and at the
beginning of Sargon's reign the king of Hamath bears a
distinctively Jewish name.   This is Yahu-bihdi, or, as
it is elsewhere written, Ilu-bihdi, where the word *ilu*,
"god," takes the place of the name of the covenant God
of Israel.   It is even possible that Yahu-bihdi was a
Jew who had been placed on the throne of Hamath by
Azariah.   At any rate, the alliance between Judah and
Hamath explains a passage in 2 Kings xiv. 28, which
has long presented a difficulty.   It is now clear that
Jeroboam is here stated to have won over Hamath to
Israel, though previously it had "been allied with Judah."
But after Jeroboam's death, Jewish influence must
once more have gained an ascendency among the
Hamathites.

Two years after the fall of Arpad, Tiglath-Pileser was
again in the west.   On this occasion he held a *levée* of
subject princes, among whom Rezon of Damascus and
Manahem of Samaria came to offer their gifts and do
homage to their sovereign lord.[1]   The tribute which
Tiglath-Pileser states that he then received from the
Israelitish king was given, according to the Book of

[1] The Assyrian inscriptions show that the true form of the name of the
king of Damascus was Rezon, like that of the founder of the kingdom
(1 Kings xi. 23), the Biblical form with *i* being due to the same vocalic
change as that in *Toi* (2 Sam. viii. 9) by the side of *Tou* (1 Chr. xviii. 9),
or Hiram (1 Kings v. 1) by the side of Huram (2 Chr. ii. 11).   Hezion
in 1 Kings xv. 18 is probably a copyist's error for Rezon.

Kings, to Pul. We may infer from this, therefore, that
the Assyrian monarch was still known to the neighbouring nations by his original name, and that it was not
until later that they became accustomed to the new title
he had assumed. The inference is further borne out by
the statement of an ancient Greek astronomer, Ptolemy.
When speaking of the eclipses which were observed at
Babylon, Ptolemy gives a list of Babylonian kings, with
the length of their reigns, from the so-called era of
Nabonassar, in B.C. 747, down to the time of Alexander
the Great. In this list, Tiglath-Pileser, after his conquest of Babylon, is named Poros or Por, Por being the
Persian form of Pul.

During the lifetime of Menahem Israel remained
tributary to Assyria, and the Assyrian king did not
again turn his arms against the west. After the death
of Menahem and the murder of his son Pekahiah, however, important changes took place. The usurper,
Pekah, in alliance with Rezon of Damascus, attacked
Judah with the intention of overthrowing the dynasty
of David and placing on the throne of Jerusalem a vassal
king whose father's name, Tabeel, shows that he must
have been a Syrian. Jotham, the Jewish king, died
shortly after the war began, and the youth and weakness of his son and successor Ahaz laid Judah open to
its antagonists, who were further aided by a disaffected
party within the capital itself (Isa. viii. 6). In his
extremity, therefore, Ahaz appealed to the Assyrian
monarch, who was already seeking an excuse for crushing Damascus, and reducing the Jewish kingdom, with
its important fortress of Jerusalem, to a condition of
vassalage. In B.C. 734, accordingly, Tiglath-Pileser
marched into Syria. Rezon was defeated in a pitched

battle, his chariots broken in pieces, his captains captured
and impaled, while he himself escaped to Damascus,
where he was closely besieged by the enemy.   The
territory of Damascus was now devastated with fire and
sword, its sixteen districts were "overwhelmed as with a
flood," and the beautiful gardens by which the capital
was surrounded were destroyed, every tree being cut
down for use in the siege.   The city itself, however,
proved too strong to be taken by assault ; so, leaving a
sufficient force before it to reduce it by famine, Tiglath-
Pileser proceeded against the late allies of the Syrian
king.   Israel was the first to be attacked.   The north of
the country was overrun, and the tribes beyond the
Jordan carried into captivity.   Gilead and Abel-beth-
maachah are mentioned by name as among the towns
that were taken and sacked.[1]   The Assyrians then fell
upon Ammon and Moab, which had aided Israel and
Syria in the attack on Judah, and next made their way
along the sea-coast into the country of the Philistines,
who had seized the opportunity of the late war to shake
off the yoke of the Jewish king.   Their leader, Khanun
or Hanno of Gaza, fled into Egypt ; but Gaza itself was
captured and laid under tribute, its gods carried away,
and an image of the Assyrian king set up in the temple
of Dagon.   Ekron and Ashdod were also punished, and
Metinti of Ashkelon committed suicide in order to escape
the vengeance of the conqueror.

Now that all fear of danger in the south had been
removed, Tiglath-Pileser marched back into the northern
kingdom, took Samaria, and (according to his own
account) put Pekah to death, appointing Hosea king in
his place.   A yearly tribute of ten talents of gold and

[1] Compare 2 Kings xv. 29.

a thousand of silver was at the same time exacted. Shortly afterwards some of the Assyrian troops were sent against the Edomites and the Queen of the Arabs, who had also revolted against Assyria and joined the Syro-Israelite league. Indeed, this league seems to have been formed for the purpose of checking the Assyrian advance, and the war against Judah to have been due to a refusal of Jotham to take part in it. It was an anticipation of the league that was afterwards formed in the time of Hezekiah against the growing power of Sargon.

Meanwhile, after a siege of two years, Damascus fell in B.C. 732. Rezon was slain, his subjects transported into captivity, and a great court, like a durbar in modern India, was held in his palace by Tiglath-Pileser. Among the subject-princes who attended it was Ahaz of Judah. He is called Jehoahaz in the Assyrian inscriptions, and it is therefore clear that the sacred historians have dropped the first part of the name, in consequence of the character of the king. The divine name would have been profaned by its association with an idolatrous and unworthy prince. As Khanun appeared at the court along with Kavus-melech of Edom, Metinti of Ashkelon, Solomon of Moab, and Sanib of Ammon, he must have succeeded in obtaining a pardon. It was while Ahaz was at Damascus in attendance on the Assyrian monarch that he saw the altar, the pattern of which he sent to Urijah, ordering it to be set up in the court of the Lord's house.

Tiglath-Pileser died in B.C. 727, and was succeeded by Shalmaneser IV. The refusal of Hosea to continue the annual tribute brought the new Assyrian monarch into the west. Tyre was besieged unsuccessfully, Hosea carried away captive, and Samaria blockaded for three years. During the blockade Shalmaneser died, and the crown was seized by one of the Assyrian generals. The latter assumed the name of Sargon, in memory of the famous Babylonian monarch who had reigned so many centuries before. The capture of Samaria took place in his first year (B.C. 722); 27,280 of its inhabitants were sent into exile, but only fifty chariots were found in the city. An Assyrian governor was appointed over it, who was commissioned to send each year to Nineveh the same tribute as that paid by Hosea. The comparatively small number of Israelites who were carried into captivity shows that Sargon contented himself with removing only those persons and their families who had taken part in the revolt against him; in fact, Samaria was treated pretty much as Jerusalem was by Nebuchadrezzar in the time of Jehoiachin. The greater part of the old population was allowed to remain in its native land. This fact disposes of the modern theories which assume that the whole of the Ten Tribes were carried away. The districts to which the captives were taken were Halah, the banks of the Habor, or river of Gozan, and the cities of the Medes. Halah was not far from Haran in Mesopotamia, on the western side of the Habor, the modern Khabur, which flows into the Euphrates, and rises in the country called Guzana, or Gozan, in the Assyrian inscriptions. The Medes were the tribes who lived eastward of Kurdistan, which, like Mesopotamia, had been overrun by Tiglath-Pileser.

The places of the captive Israelites were not supplied immediately. We learn from the Old Testament that it was from Hamath and the cities of Babylonia that the new inhabitants were brought. Now Hamath was not conquered by Sargon until B.C. 720, and Babylonia not until B.C. 710.   Hamath had broken into revolt under Yahu-bihdi or Ilu-bihdi, who induced Arpad, Damascus, and Samaria to follow its example.   But its chastisement was speedy and sharp.   Sargon captured Ilu-bihdi in the city of Aroer, and flayed him alive ; while Hamath received a colony of 4,300 Assyrians and an Assyrian governor.   Samaria was next punished, and Sargon then marched southward against the combined forces of Khanun of Gaza and Sabako or So of Egypt.   A battle at Raphia decided the fate of the struggle, and Khanun fell into the hands of his enemies.

The Babylonian cities from which some of the new settlers in Samaria were taken were Cuthah and Sepharvaim.   Cuthah is now represented by the mounds of Tel Ibrahim, to the north-west of Babylon. . It was under the special protection of Nergal, whose name means "the lord of the great city," the god of the underworld.   Sepharvaim, or "the two Sipparas," stood on opposite banks of the Euphrates.   The quarter on the eastern bank, now called Abu-Habba, was Sippara proper, where, according to Babylonian tradition, Sisuthros had buried his books before the Deluge; the quarter on the other bank being Agadé or Accad, the old capital of Sargon I, which gave its name to the whole of the northern portion of Chaldea.   In later times the two quarters were distinguished from one another as "Sippara of Samas," the Sun-god, and "Sippara of Anunit."   Anunit was the wife of the god Anu, "the sky"; and when the Bible says that "the Sepharvites burnt their children in fire to Anammelech" reference is made to "Anu the king."   Adrammelech, or "Adar the king," was another Babylonian deity, who was originally a form of the Sun-god.

We may gather from Ezra iv. 2, 10, that Samaria was colonised a second time by the Assyrians, perhaps in consequence of an unsuccessful revolt. This took place in the reign of Esar-haddon. His son Asnapper, or Assur-bani-pal, settled a number of Elamite tribes in the country, among them being natives of Susa and of Apharsa or Mal Amir. Men from Babylon and Erech were also settled there at the same time. The names of the new colonists would suit the reign of Assur-bani-pal better than that of Esar-haddon, since it was Assur-bani-pal, and not Esar-haddon, who conquered Elam and Susa, and took by storm both Babylon and Erech. It is, therefore, probable that Esar-haddon in verse 2 is a scribe's error for Asnapper.

The reduction of the northern kingdom of Israel into an Assyrian province brought the Assyrian empire to the very borders of Judah, and the Assyrian kings began to cast longing eyes upon the territory of the latter. Its capital, Jerusalem, was an almost impregnable fortress, the possession of which would open the road into Egypt, as well as block the passage of an Egyptian army into Asia. But as yet there was no excuse for attacking it. Hezekiah, the successor of Ahaz, continued to pay the tribute his father had consented to give to the Assyrians, and Sargon accordingly occupied himself in wars elsewhere. Suddenly, however, an event occurred which brought him once more into Palestine. In order to understand this, we must turn our eyes for a moment or two to Babylonia.

The Babylonians had seized the opportunity offered by the death of Tiglath-Pileser to shake off the Assyrian yoke. For five years they remained free. Then in B.C. 722 the country was occupied by a man of

great energy and ability, Merodach-baladan, the son of
Yagina.¹   Merodach-baladan was the hereditary chief
of the Kaldâ or Chaldeans, a small tribe at that time
settled in the marshes at the mouth of the Euphrates,
but which, in consequence of his conquest of Babylon
afterwards, became the dominant caste in Babylonia
itself.   For twelve years he continued undisputed master
of the country we may henceforth call Chaldea.   Sargon,
however, was becoming every year more powerful, and it
was evident that another Assyrian invasion of Babylonia
would   not   be   long   postponed.   Merodach-baladan
determined   to   anticipate   the   attack.   He   therefore
endeavoured to form a vast league between the states on
both the eastern and the western sides of the Assyrian
empire, whose independence was menaced by their
powerful neighbour.   Babylonia and Elam were the
eastern members of the league, and ambassadors were
sent to the west, to concert measures with the various
states of Palestine, as well as with Egypt, for common
action against Sargon.

Hezekiah, now in the fourteenth year of his reign
(2 Kings xx. 6), had just recovered from a dangerous
illness, which had been aggravated by the fear of
Assyria, and the fact that as yet he had no son
to succeed him.   The illness formed the pretext by
which the conspirators hoped to blind the eyes of
Sargon to the real objects of the embassy; it was
published to the world that the ambassadors had come

---

¹ The name of Baladan in 2 Kings xx. 12 (and Isa. xxxix. 1) is due to
the error of a copyist, like Berodach for Merodach.   His eye must have
run back to the name of Merodach-baladan in the preceding line.   Merodach-baladan means " Merodach has given a son," and without " Merodach "
would be incomplete.

merely to congratulate the Jewish king on his recovery.
But Sargon knew well that Merodach-baladan would not
have troubled himself to enquire after the health of a
brother-king without a further motive, and he doubtless
learned that Hezekiah had shown the ambassadors all
the treasures and arms with which he hoped to support
the league. The consequence was, that before the confederates were prepared to resist him, the Assyrian
monarch had swooped down upon them and attacked
them singly.

Palestine was the first to suffer. Akhimit, whom
Sargon had appointed king of Ashdod, had been dethroned, and the crown given to an usurper named
Yavan or "the Greek." Yavan seems to have been the
nominee of Hezekiah, who at this time exercised a sort
of suzerainty over the Philistine cities, and he was set
up as king for the purpose of heading the Philistine
revolt against Assyria. Edom and Moab also sent
contingents to the war, and the Ethiopian king of Egypt
promised help. Of the details of the struggle between
Sargon and the western states we unfortunately know
nothing. But it did not last long; neither Babylonia
nor Egypt had time to send any assistance to their
allies. The *Tartan* or Commander-in-chief was ordered
to invest Ashdod (see Isa. xx. 1), while Sargon himself
overran "the wide-spreading land of Judah," and captured its capital Jerusalem. This conquest of Judah by
Sargon explains prophecies of Isaiah which have
hitherto been unsolved mysteries. Thus an explanation
is at length offered of the circumstances described by the
prophet in chapters x. and xi. Here the Assyrian army
is described as marching along the usual high-road from
the north-east, and as halting at Nob, only an hour's

journey distant from Jerusalem, on the very day when the oracle was uttered,[1] while Isaiah declares that the capital itself shall fall into the hands of the enemy (x. 6, 12, 22, 24, 34).

All this is inapplicable to the invasion of Sennacherib, when a detachment only of the Assyrian army was sent against Jerusalem from the south-west, and when Isaiah was commissioned by God to promise that the king of Assyria should "not come into this city, nor shoot an arrow there, nor come before it with shield, nor cast a bank against it." The older commentators were accordingly driven to the desperate expedient of supposing that the invasion described by Isaiah in the tenth chapter of his prophecies was an ideal one. Thanks, however, to the decipherment of the cuneiform inscriptions, all is now clear, and we can now understand why it is that the Assyrian monarch, whose march is described by Isaiah, claims to be the conqueror of Calno and Carchemish, of Hamath and Arpad, of Damascus and Samaria (vv. 8–10). All these were conquests of Sargon, not of Sennacherib.

Ashdod was taken and razed to the ground, and its inhabitants sold into captivity. Yavan managed to escape to the Egyptian king, who was cowardly enough to give him up to his enemies. Edom and Moab were punished for the part they had taken in the rebellion, and the authority of Sargon was paramount as far as the frontier of Egypt.

All this happened in B.C. 711. The following year the whole power of Assyria was hurled against Merodach-baladan. The Elamites were defeated and their

---

[1] "That day" in the A. V. should be corrected into "to-day" (Isa. x. 32).

border-towns sacked, and the Babylonian king was compelled to retreat southwards, leaving Babylon in the hands of the Assyrians.   A year later he was pursued by Sargon into his last refuge; Bit-Yagina, his ancestral capital, was taken by storm, and he himself forced to surrender.   His good fortune never returned.   On Sargon's death he once more entered Babylon, but his second reign only lasted six months.   After a battle which ended in the complete victory of Sennacherib, he fled again to the marshes, but was driven out of them four years later, and sailed across the Persian Gulf to find a new home on the western coast of Elam.   But even here his implacable enemies followed him.   In B.C. 697, Sennacherib manned a fleet with Phœnician sailors and destroyed the town the old Chaldean prince had built.   After this we hear of him no more.

The tenth chapter of Isaiah teaches us to look for references to the capture of Jerusalem by Sargon in other parts of the book.   It is impossible not to recognise one of these in the twenty-second chapter. Here the prophet presents us with the picture of a siege which has already lasted some time, and when the inhabitants of Jerusalem are no longer slain by the sword, but by famine, while the city is on the point of being starved out.   Here also the message which Isaiah is bidden to deliver is not a promise of deliverance from the enemy, but the reverse: "It was revealed in my ears by the Lord of Hosts, surely this iniquity shall not be purged from you till ye die, saith the Lord God of Hosts."   It is only the campaign of Sargon that can explain these words.

Ten years later Judah was again invaded by an Assyrian king, and Jerusalem again threatened by an

Assyrian army.   Sargon had been murdered by his soldiers, and succeeded by his son, Sennacherib, who mounted the throne on the 12th of the month of Ab, or July, B.C. 705.   He was a very different man from his father, weak and vain-glorious, fonder of boasting than of deeds.   Trusting to the support of Tirhakah, the Ethiopian king of Egypt, Hezekiah threw off his allegiance to Assyria, and refused to send the yearly tribute to Nineveh.   The Phœnicians did the same, while the Jewish king reasserted his former supremacy over the cities of the Philistines.   Padi, the king of Ekron, who remained faithful to Assyria, was carried in chains to Jerusalem, and Zedekiah, who is named in the Assyrian records as the king of Ashkelon, was probably of Jewish origin.   It was not until three years after his accession that Sennacherib found himself able to march against the rebels.   In B.C. 701 he crossed the Euphrates, and made his way to the shores of the Mediterranean.   Great and Little Sidon, Sarepta, Acre, and other Phœnician towns, surrendered to the invader, the Sidonian monarch fled to Cyprus, and the kings of Arvad and Gebal hastened to pay their court to the conquerer.   Metinti of Ashdod, Pedael of Ammon, Chemosh-nadad of Moab, and Melech-ram of Edom, who were also suspected of having taken part in the rebellion, came at the same time.   Judah and the dependent Philistine states alone still held out.

The rest of the history had best be told in Sennacherib's own words.   "Zedekiah, king of Ashkelon," he says, "who had not submitted to my yoke, himself, the gods of the house of his fathers, his wife, his sons, his daughters and his brothers, the seed of the house of his fathers, I removed, and I sent him to Assyria.   I set over the men of Ashkelon, Sarludari, the son of Rukipti, their former king, and I imposed upon him the payment of tribute, and the homage due to my majesty, and he became a vassal.   In the course of my campaign I approached and captured Beth-Dagon, Joppa, Bene-berak and Azur, the cities of Zedekiah, which did not submit at once to my yoke, and I carried away their spoil.   The priests, the chief men, and the common people of Ekron, who had thrown into chains their king Padi because he was faithful to his oaths to Assyria, and had given him up to Hezekiah, the Jew, who imprisoned him like an enemy in a dark dungeon, feared in their hearts.   The king of Egypt, the bowmen, the chariots and the horses of the king of Ethiopia, had gathered together innumerable forces and gone to their assist-ance.   In sight of the town of Eltekeh was their order of battle drawn up; they called their troops (to the battle).   Trusting in Assur, my lord, I fought with them and overthrew them.   My hands took the captains of the chariots and the sons of the king of Egypt, as well as the captains of the chariots of the king of Ethiopia, alive in the midst of the battle.   I approached and captured the towns of Eltekeh and Timnath, and I carried away their spoil.   I marched against the city of Ekron, and put to death the priests and the chief men who had committed the sin (of rebellion), and I hung up their bodies on stakes all round the city.   The citizens who had done wrong and wickedness I counted as a spoil; as for the rest of them who had done no sin or crime, in whom no fault was found, I proclaimed their freedom (from punishment).   I had Padi, their king, brought out from the midst of Jerusalem, and I seated him on the throne of royalty over them, and I laid upon him the tribute due to my majesty. But as for Hezekiah of Judah, who had not submitted to my yoke, forty-six of his strong cities, together with innumerable fortresses and small towns which depended on them, by overthrowing the walls and open attack, by battle, engines and battering-rams I besieged, I captured. I brought out from the midst of them and counted as a spoil 200,150 persons, great and small, male and female, horses, mules, asses, camels, oxen and sheep without number. Hezekiah himself I shut up like a bird in a cage in Jerusalem, his royal city. I built a line of forts against him, and I kept back his heel from going forth out of the great gate of his city. I cut off his cities which I had spoiled from the midst of his land, and gave them to Metinti, king of Ashdod, Padi, king of Ekron, and Zil-baal, king of Gaza, and I made his country small. In addition to their former tribute and yearly gifts I added other tribute, and the homage due to my majesty, and I laid it upon them. The fear of the greatness of my majesty overwhelmed him, even Hezekiah, and he sent after me to Nineveh, my royal city, by way of gift and tribute, the Arabs and his body-guard whom he had brought for the defence of Jerusalem, his royal city, and had furnished with pay, along with thirty talents of gold, 800 talents of pure silver, carbuncles and other precious stones, a couch of ivory, thrones of ivory, an elephant's hide, an elephant's tusk, rare woods, whatever their names, a vast treasure, as well as the eunuchs of his palace, dancing men and dancing women; and he sent his ambassador to offer homage."

The Assyrian and the Biblical accounts complete and supplement one another. Sennacherib naturally glosses

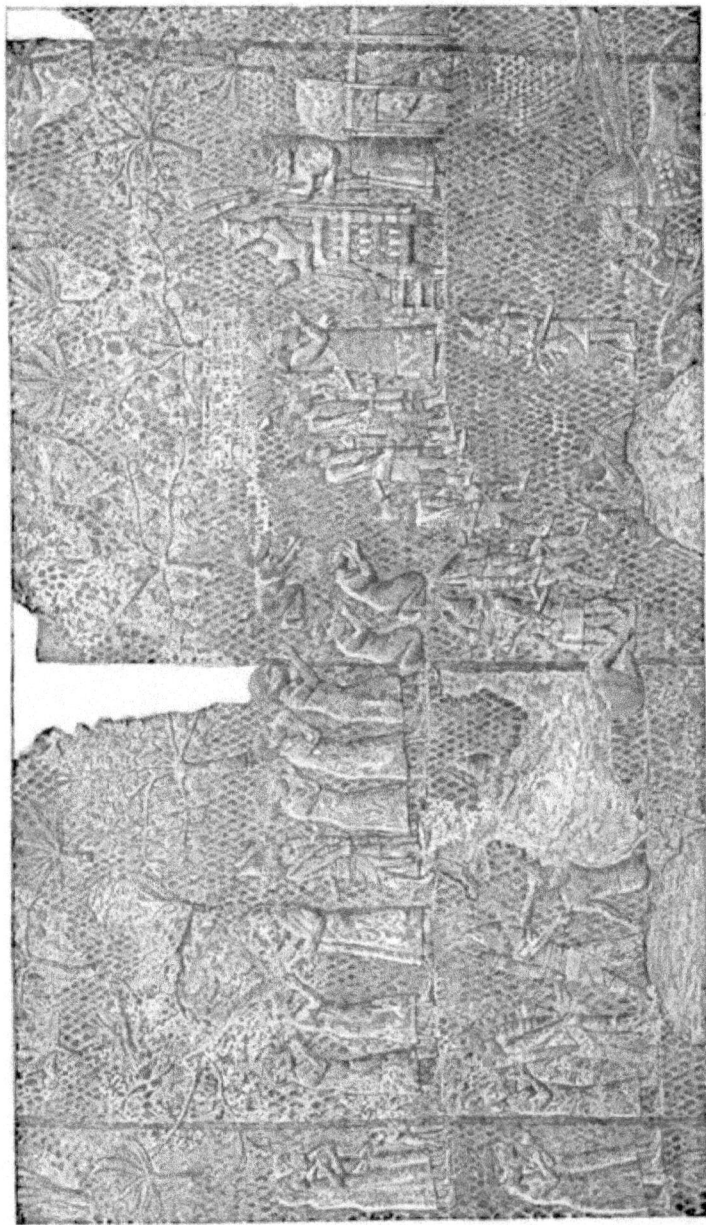

Assyrian sculpture representing the capture of Lachish by Sennacherib. The inscription reads : " Sennacherib, the king of multitudes, the king of Assyria, sat on an upright throne, and the spoil of the city of Lachish passed before him."

over the disaster that befel him in Palestine, and transfers the payment of the tribute from the time when Hezekiah vainly hoped to buy off the siege of Jerusalem to the end of the campaign.   But he cannot conceal the fact that he never succeeded in taking the revolted city or in punishing Hezekiah, as he had punished other rebel kings, nor did he again undertake a campaign in the west.   We find him the next year in Babylonia ; then he attacked the tribes of Cilicia ; but he never again ventured into Palestine.   During the rest of his lifetime Judah had nothing more to fear from the Assyrian king.

At first sight there seems to be a discrepancy between the number of silver talents stated in the Bible to have been paid by Hezekiah, and the number which Sennacherib claims to have received.   But the discrepancy is only an apparent one.   It has been shown that there were two standards of value, according to one of which 500 talents of silver would be equivalent to 800 talents, if reckoned by the other.   A more real discrepancy is to be found in the statement of Sennacherib that he had built a line of forts round about Jerusalem, and prevented Hezekiah from getting out of it.   This is in flagrant contradiction to the words of Isaiah, that the Assyrian king should not shoot an arrow into Jerusalem, nor assault it under the cover of shields, nor cast a bank against it.   Sennacherib claims to have performed more than he actually did.

Another discrepancy has been found in the date assigned by the Biblical narrative to the Assyrian invasion.   The year B.C. 701 was the twenty-fourth year of Hezekiah, not the fourteenth, which fell in B.C. 711, the year of Sargon's campaign.   But this very fact supplies an explanation of the difficulty.   In the retrospective record of the prophetical annalist, the two campaigns of Sargon and Sennacherib have been brought into association, though the history dwells only upon that one which illustrated God's way of dealing with His faithful servants.   Hence it is that reminiscences of the earlier invasion are allowed to enter here and there into the narrative.   It was Sargon, and not Sennacherib, who was the conqueror of Hamath and Arpad, of Sepharvaim and Samaria (2 Kings xviii. 34– 36).   It was Sargon, and not Sennacherib, who invaded Judah in the fourteenth year of Hezekiah's reign.

There is a bas-relief in the British Museum which represents Sennacherib seated on his throne in front of Lachish, and receiving the spoil of the city as it passed before him.   It was while he was encamped before this city that Hezekiah despatched the embassy with gifts and tribute and prayers for pardon.   Sennacherib accepted the gifts, but refused the pardon ; nothing would content him but the absolute surrender of Jerusalem and its king.   Hezekiah then prepared for his defence.   We gather from Isaiah's writings that there were at that period three parties in the State, each of which at different times gained an influence over the king and his councillors.   There was first the party headed by Shebna—whose name proves him to have been of Syrian parentage—which advocated alliance with Egypt and hostility to Assyria.   This was the party with which Isaiah had mainly to contend, but its power was not finally extinguished until after the retreat of Tirhakah from the battle of Eltekeh, and this visible proof that Egypt was but a bruised reed to lean upon.   The second party inherited the policy of Ahaz, and urged that Judah's only chance of safety lay in submission to the mighty Empire of Assyria. Isaiah was the representative of the third party. He announced God's own declaration, that He would defend His city and temple if only its inhabitants would trust and fear Him, and reject all alliances with the heathen nations that surrounded them. "In quietness and in confidence" should be their strength. It was not until events had demonstrated the truth of Isaiah's message that the rulers of Jerusalem reluctantly accepted it, and recognised at last that the true policy of Judah was to abstain from mixing in the wars and intrigues of the foreign idolater.

When the Jewish embassy arrived at Lachish, the Egyptian party seems still to have been in the ascendant. In spite of the prophet's warning, envoys had been sent to Egypt (Isa. xxx. xxxi.), and had returned full of confidence in an alliance, which yet was to be to them not "an help nor profit, but a shame and also a reproach." The battle of Eltekeh dissipated their hopes. This was fought after the capture of Lachish, when Sennacherib was endeavouring to take the neighbouring fortress of Libnah (2 Kings xix. 8, 9). The Rab-shakeh or Prime Minister had been sent against Jerusalem along with the Tartan or Commander-in-chief and the Rab-saris or Chamberlain, and after delivering his message to its defenders had returned to Sennacherib, leaving a considerable force under the Tartan encamped outside its walls. The message had been delivered in Hebrew, not in Assyrian or in Aramaic (Syrian), which at that time was the general language of trade and diplomacy in Western Asia, like French in modern Europe. Every politician was expected to speak it, and Hezekiah's ministers take it for granted that the Rab-shakeh would be able to do so. The fact that he preferred to speak in Hebrew gives us a high idea of the education of the age. Every cultivated Assyrian was acquainted with Accadian, the old dead language of Babylonia, which was to an Assyrian what Latin is to us; and in addition to this diplomatists and men of business were required to know Aramaic, while we here find the highest of Assyrian officials further able to converse in Hebrew.

A reminiscence of the disaster which befel the Assyrian army was preserved in an Egyptian legend, which ascribed it to the piety of an Egyptian king. Influenced by this legend, some scholars have supposed that it took place at Pelusium, on the Egyptian frontier; but the language of Scripture seems hardly to leave a doubt that it really happened before Jerusalem. The result was the abrupt breaking up of the Assyrian camp and the termination of the siege of Jerusalem. Sennacherib hastened back to Nineveh, and the court annalists were bidden to draw a veil of silence over the conclusion of the campaign.

Hezekiah did not long survive his wonderful deliverance. Next to Solomon he seems to have been the most cultivated of the Jewish kings. His public works rendered Jerusalem one of the most formidable fortresses of the ancient world; and if the tunnel of Siloam belongs to his reign, it is clear that he had at his disposal engineering skill of a high order. He was not only himself a poet, but a restorer of the old psalmody and a patron of literature. In imitation, probably, of the libraries of Assyria and Babylonia, he established a library in Jerusalem, where scribes were employed, as they were at Nineveh, in making new editions of ancient works (see Prov. xxv. 1.). Ahaz had introduced into Judah the study of astronomy, for which the Babylonians were renowned, and had set up a gnomon or sun-dial in the palace-court (2 Kings xx. 11). It is possible that some of the astronomical literature of Babylonia, which has been recovered from the cuneiform tablets now in the British Museum, was introduced at the same time, with its multitudinous observations and prediction of eclipses, its notices of the appearance of comets, of the movements of the planets and fixed stars, of the phases of Venus, and even of spots on the sun. It is also possible that the Assyrian calendar and the Assyrian names of the months now first became familiar to the Jews. At any rate, it would seem, from Jer. xxxii. 10, 11, that clay came to be used in Judah as a writing material, just as it was at Babylon or Nineveh, the inner clay record of a contract being covered with an outer coating, on which was inscribed an abstract of its contents, together with the names of the witnesses. Jeremiah's deed of purchase, moreover, was preserved in a jar, like the numerous clay deeds of the Egibi banking-firm, which existed at Babylon from the age of Nebuchadrezzar to that of Xerxes. These jars served the purpose of our modern safes.

Sennacherib lived for twenty years after his withdrawal from Palestine. In B.C. 681 he was murdered by his two elder sons, Adar-melech and Nergal-sharezer, who were jealous of the favour shown by him towards their younger brother Esar-haddon. A curious evidence of this favour exists among the tablets in the British Museum. This is nothing less than the will of Sennacherib, made apparently some years before his death, in which he bequeaths to Esar-haddon certain private pro-

perty. The document reads as follows:—"I, Sennacherib, king of multitudes, king of Assyria, bequeath
armlets of gold, quantities of ivory, a platter of gold,
ornaments, and chains for the neck, all these beautiful
things of which there are heaps, and three sorts of precious stones, one and a half manehs and two and a half
shekels in weight, to Esar-haddon my son, whose name
was afterwards changed to Assur-sar-illik-pal by my wish.
The treasure is deposited in the house of Amuk." The
king was excused the necessity of having his will
attested by witnesses, as was obligatory in the case of
other persons; and it is plain that at the time when it
was made Esar-haddon was not the recognised heir to
the throne.

The murder of the old king took place, according to
the Bible, "as he was worshipping in the house of Nisroch
his god." The reading of the god's name, however, is
corrupt, since no such deity was known to the Assyrians,
and it is possible that Nusku, the companion of Nebo,
the patron of literature, is intended. A war was going
on at the time between Assyria and Armenia, and the
murderers finding, apparently, no adherents in Nineveh,
fled to Erimenas, the Armenian king. Esar-haddon, at
the head of the Assyrian veterans, met them and the
Armenian forces, a few weeks afterwards, at a place not
far from Melitene, the modern Malatiyeh, in Kappadokia.
The battle ended in the complete victory of the Assyrians,
and Esar-haddon was saluted "king" on the spot by
his soldiers. He then returned to Nineveh, and there
formally ascended the throne.

Esar-haddon resembled his father but little. He was
one of the ablest generals Assyria ever produced, and
was distinguished from his predecessors by his mild and

conciliatory policy. Under him the Assyrian empire reached its furthest limits, Egypt being conquered, and placed under twenty Assyrian satraps, while an Assyrian army penetrated into the very heart of the Arabian desert. But the conquests which had been won in war were cemented by a policy of justice and moderation. Thus Babylon, which had been razed to the ground by Sennacherib in B.C. 691, and the adjoining river choked with its ruins, was rebuilt, and Esar-haddon endeavoured to win over the Babylonians by residing in it during half the year. This affords an explanation of a fact mentioned in the Second Book of Chronicles (xxxiii. 11), which has long been a stumbling-block in the way of critics. It is there said that the king of Assyria, after crushing the revolt of Manasseh, carried him away captive to Babylon. The cause of this is now clear. As Esar-haddon spent part of his time at Babylon it merely depended on the season of the year to which of his two capitals, Nineveh or Babylon, a political prisoner should be brought. The treatment of Manasseh was in full accordance with the treatment of other rebel princes in the time of Esar-haddon's son, Assur-bani-pal. Like them, he was at first loaded with chains, but was afterwards allowed to return to his kingdom and reinstated in the government of it.

The name of " Manasseth, king of Judah," twice occurs on the Assyrian monuments. Once he is mentioned among the tributaries of Esar-haddon, once among those of Assur bani-pal. It is clear, therefore, that at some period shortly after Hezekiah's death, Judah was again forced to pay tribute and do homage to the Assyrian king. When Esar-haddon passed through Palestine on his way to Egypt, he found there only submission and

I

respect.　Sidon alone withstood him, and Sidon was
accordingly destroyed.

The "burden" pronounced upon Egypt by Isaiah
(ch. xix.) must belong to the age of Esar-haddon.　The
condition of Egypt at the time was exactly that
described by the prophet.　The country was divided
into hostile kingdoms, which fought "every one against
his brother, and every one against his neighbour; city
against city, and kingdom against kingdom."　Tirhakah
the Ethiopian, whom the Assyrians had driven out,
invaded it from the south, and Esar-haddon came down
upon it from the north.　He it is who is "the fierce
king" who, the Lord declared, should rule over the
Egyptians.　For about twenty years the unhappy country
was wasted with fire and sword.　The twenty governors
appointed by the Assyrians were constantly intriguing
against one another and their suzerain; and again and
again the Assyrian armies were called upon to return to
Egypt to suppress a revolt.　It was during one of these
campaigns—that which happened about B.C. 665, in the
reign of Assur-bani-pal—that Thebes, the ancient capital
of Upper Egypt, was destroyed.　It is termed Ni in the
Assyrian texts, a name which corresponds to the Hebrew
No-Amon, or No of Amun, the supreme god of the city.
Its temples and palaces were overthrown, their treasures
were carried away, and two obelisks, which together
weighed over seventy tons, were sent as trophies to
Nineveh.　Nahum (iii. 8) alludes to this destruction of
Thebes as a recent event, and thus fixes the approximate
age of his life and ministry.

The reign of Esar-haddon was a short one.　In
B.C. 670, on the 12th day of Iyyar, or April, he convened
by edict a great assembly in Nineveh, and there asso-

ciated his son Assur-bani-pal, whom the Greeks called
Sardanapalus, in the government. Two years later he
died, and Assur-bani-pal was proclaimed sole king on
the 27th of Ab, or July. Assur-bani-pal, the *grand
monarque* of Assyria, whose long reign was a continuous
series of wars, and building, and magnificent patronage of
art and literature, has little direct contact with Biblical
history. The conquest of Elam by his generals removed
the last civilized power which could struggle with
Assyria; but it was not fully accomplished when the
mighty empire began to totter to its fall. A general
rebellion broke out, at the heart of which was Assur-
bani-pal's own brother, the viceroy of Babylonia. All
the strength of Assyria was spent in crushing it; and
Egypt, which had revolted through the help of Gyges of
Lydia, was never reconquered. Palestine, strangely
enough, seems to have been but little affected by the
almost universal outbreak; indeed, Chemosh-khalta of
Moab materially assisted Assur-bani-pal, by defeating
the Kedarites and sending their sheikh in chains to
Nineveh. One or two Phœnician cities alone took
occasion to refuse their tribute. We do not know the
year of Assur-bani-pal's death, but it was probably about
B.C. 630. He left a troubled heritage to his successors.
The viceroy of Babylonia was becoming more and more
independent; Elam, the latest Assyrian conquest, was
threatened by the Persians, and a new and ferocious
enemy had appeared in the north. These were the
Scythians, who had descended upon the civilised world
from the steppes of Southern Russia. They extended
their ravages as far as Palestine, and their occupation of
Beth-Shan caused it to be known in later days as
Scythopolis, "the city of the Scythians." The earlier

prophecies of Jeremiah refer to the miseries inflicted on
the country by these barbarians, who must have entered
it towards the middle of Josiah's reign. By this time
the authority of Assyria in the west could have been but
nominal.   Nineveh itself had undergone a siege at the
hands of the Medes, and was only saved from utter
destruction by the Scythian irruption. Hence we can
understand how it was that Josiah was able to re-unite
the monarchy of David, and extend his sway over what
had once been the kingdom of Samaria.   There was no
longer an Assyrian governor to forbid his overthrowing
the altar at Bethel or the "houses of the high places
that were in the cities of Samaria."

The date of the final fall and destruction of Nineveh
is not certain, and much depends on the interpretation
given to the words "the king of Assyria" in 2 Kings
xxiii. 29.   If, as is usually supposed, these really signify
the king of Babylon, who had succeeded to the power
of Assyria, we may place the fall of the Assyrian
capital in B.C. 610; otherwise the date must be as late
as B.C. 606.   It cannot be later, since, when Jeremiah
reviews in this year the existing nations of the east
(xxv. 19–26), he says not a word about either Nineveh
or Assyria.   The vengeance the prophets had predicted
for the Assyrians had already fallen upon them.   What
it was to be like we may gather from the language of
Nahum.

The last king of Assyria was Esar-haddon II, called
Sarakos by the Greek writers.   He has left us a few
records, which were written when his enemies were
gathering about him, and when his people were vainly
calling upon their gods for help.   The Medes, the Minni,
the Kimmerians or Gomer, had all banded themselves

together, and were steadily approaching Nineveh. The frontier cities had been stormed, and the enemy was spreading like an inundation over the whole country. In their despair the Assyrian rulers ordained a solemn fast of 100 days and 100 nights, and besought the Sun-god to pardon their sin. But all was in vain. The measure of the iniquities of Assyria was filled up; the time had come when the desolater should himself be desolate, and Nineveh, as God's prophets had threatened, was laid utterly waste.[1]

[1] The following chronological table will enable the reader to understand without difficulty the order of the events described in the preceding chapter :—

B.C.

1130. Reign of Tiglath-Pileser I, in Assyria : campaigns in Syria and Cilicia.

900. Recovery of Assyria after a period of decline.

858. Accession of Shalmaneser II.

853. Battle of Karkar.

851. Death of Ahab.

850. Campaign of Shalmaneser against Hadadezer (Ben-hadad II).

845. Campaign against Hadadezer.

843. Murder of Hadadezer by Hazael.

841. Campaign against Hazael ; tribute paid to Shalmaneser by Jehu.

823. Shalmaneser II succeeded by Samas-Rimmon.

810. Samas-Rimmon succeeded by Rimmon-nirari.

804. Damascus captured by the Assyrians : tribute paid by Samaria.

781. Rimmon-nirari succeeded by Shalmaneser III.

773 Campaign against Damascus.

745. April. Pul, who takes the name of Tiglath-Pileser II, usurps the Assyrian throne.

743-40. War with Hamath ; submission of Uzziah ; fall of Arpad.

738. Tribute paid to the Assyrians by Menahem and Rezon.

734. Damascus besieged ; the tribes beyond the Jordan carried away ; Jehoahaz (Ahaz) of Judah becomes an Assyrian vassal.

733 (? 729). Pekah put to death ; Hosea succeeds.

732. Damascus taken ; Rezon slain. Ahaz at Damascus.

727. Tiglath-Pileser succeeded by Shalmaneser IV.

722. Sargon seizes the throne and captures Samaria.

721. Merodach-baladan conquers Babylonia.

B.C.

720. Hamath conquered ; Sabako (So) of Egypt defeated at Raphia

712. Embassy of Merodach-baladan to Hezekiah.

711. Capture of Jerusalem and Ashdod by Sargon.

710. Merodach-baladan driven from Babylonia.

705. Murder of Sargon ; his son Sennacherib succeeds on the 12th of Ab.

704. Merodach-baladan holds Babylon for six months.

701. Campaign against Judah ; battle of Eltekeh ; retreat of Sennacherib from Jerusalem.

681. Murder of Sennacherio ; accession of Esar-haddon.

676. Manasseh appears among the Assyrian tributaries. Egypt conquered.

670. Assur-bani-pal (Sardanapalus) associated in the government on the 12th of Iyyar.

668. Esar-haddon dies ; Assur-bani-pal succeeds on the 27th of Ab.

665. Destruction of Thebes (No-Amun) by the Assyrians.

?606. Fall of Nineveh, Esar-haddon II or Sarakos being the last king.

CHAPTER VII.

NEBUCHADREZZAR AND CYRUS.

Rise of the Babylonian empire.—Media.—Pharaoh-Necho.—The battle of Carchemish.—Nebuchadrezzar ascends the throne.—The splendour of Babylon.—No monuments yet discovered recording Nebuchadrezzar's Jewish and Syrian campaigns.—Evil-Merodach.—Clay documents recently discovered in Babylonia.—New light thrown on the empire of Cyrus.—The cylinder of Cyrus.—Cyrus not a monotheist.—The Babylonian King of Isaiah xiv.—Cyrus not a King of Persia at all.—Babylon not besieged by Cyrus.—How Cyrus came to let the Jews return.—Correspondence between the language of Cyrus and of Scripture.—" The god who raises the dead to life."—Prayer after a bad dream.—Babylonian penitential psalms.—A translation of one of them.—Chronological table of the events of the chapter.

THE empire of Babylonia arose out of the ashes of the empire of Assyria. While the bands of the enemy were gathering round the doomed city of Nineveh, Nabopolassar, the viceroy of Babylonia, seized the opportunity for revolt. There were no armies now, as in former days, that could pour out of the gates of the Assyrian capital to punish the rebel, and Nabopolassar was allowed to establish his new monarchy undisturbed. But the fall of the imperial city left the other provinces of the Assyrian empire without a master or a defence. Its latest conquest, Elam, seems to have recovered its independence for a short time—at all events, Jeremiah (xxv. 25) in the year 606 B.C. speaks of "the kings of Elam"—but elsewhere its possessions became the battleground of the three rival powers of Babylon, of Media, and of Egypt.

Media was the name given by Persian and Greek writers to the kingdom 'of Ekbatana, a city now represented by Hamadan. Its native name, at all events in the time of Sargon, was Ellip, and the title of Media applied to it in later history seems to have been due to a confusion between the Assyrian words *Madâ* "Medes," and *Manda*, "barbarian." As we shall see, Astyages, the king of Ekbatana, is called "the king of the people of *Manda*," or "barbarians," by the Babylonian king Nabonidos. The tablets which describe the approach of the last enemies of Nineveh draw a careful distinction between Kaztarit, or Kyaxares, "lord of the city of Car-Cassi," and Mamiti-arsu, "lord of the city of the Medes." For the Assyrians, the Medes were only the small tribes which inhabited the regions eastward of Kurdistan. The error, however, which turned the kingdom of Ekbatana into a kingdom of Media has fixed itself in literature, and the Old Testament also has adopted in regard to it the current language of the day. It is now too late to disturb the time-honoured title, and we shall therefore continue to speak of a Median empire and a Median kingdom, even though we now know that the terms rest on an ancient mistake.

As the power of Assyria had dwindled, the power of Egypt had increased. The Egyptian kings began to dream again of an Asiatic empire, such as they had once held in days long gone by, and their first efforts were directed towards securing afresh the cities of the Philistines. Gaza and Ashdod were captured after a long siege;[1] Cyprus became an Egyptian province, and Pharaoh Necho, whose Phœnician fleet had circumnavigated Africa, set about the task of conquering Asia.

[1] See Jer. xlvii. 1.

Josiah was now on the throne of Judah. He still called himself a vassal of Assyria, and could not but see with alarm the rise of a new enemy, just as the old one had ceased to be formidable. In the name of his suzerain, therefore, he attempted to bar the advance of Necho; the two armies of Egypt and Judah met on the plain of Megiddo, where the battle ended in the death of the Jewish king and the slaughter of the flower of the Jewish soldiery. The death of Josiah proved an irremediable disaster to the Jewish state. He left behind him a family torn by jealousies and supported by rival factions, a people hostile to the religious reforms he had carried through, and an army which had lost both its leader and its veterans. From henceforth Judah was no longer able to defend itself from an invader, whether Egyptian or Babylonian; and even the strong walls of Jerusalem no longer proved a defence in days when the method of warfare had changed, and a victorious army was content to sit down for years before a fortress until its defenders had been starved out.

Necho's triumph, however, was short-lived. Three years after the battle of Megiddo (B.C. 606), he had to meet the Babylonian army, under its young general Nebuchadrezzar, the son of Nabopolassar, at the ford of the Euphrates, which was protected by the old Hittite city of Carchemish. Nabopolassar was now independent king of Babylonia, and his son had given evidence of great military capacities. He had disputed with the Median kingdom of Ekbatana the possession of Mesopotamia; and though the ruins of Nineveh and other Assyrian cities on the eastern bank of the Tigris continued to remain in the hands of the Median ruler, as well as the high road which led across Northern

Mesopotamia into Asia Minor, and passed through the patriarchal city of Haran, he had secured for his father the southern regions enclosed between the Tigris and the Euphrates. The battle of Carchemish finally decided who should be the master of Western Asia. The Egyptian forces were completely shattered, and Necho retreated with the wreck of his army to his ancestral kingdom. Judah and the countries which adjoined it passed under the yoke of Babylonia.

Two years later, in B.C. 604, Nabopolassar died, and Nebuchadrezzar succeeded to the throne. His name is written Nabu-kudur-uzur, " O Nebo, defend the crown," in the cuneiform, so that the form Nebuchadrezzar, which is found in the Book of Jeremiah, is the only correct one, Nebuchadnezzar being a corruption of it, like Asnapper for Assur-bani-pal. Nebuchadrezzar was not only a great general, he was also a great builder and an able administrator. Under him, Babylon, which had been little more than a provincial town, became one of the most splendid cities in the ancient world. In the middle of it rose the gigantic temple of Bel or Baal, in eight stages, now represented by a mound of ruins, which goes under the name of Babil. A winding road led from the foot of it to the shrine on the summit, wherein was a golden image of the god, forty feet high, and a golden table in front of it for the showbread. Nebuchadrezzar's palace, now called the Kasr mound, was on a scale equally vast, though the wall that surrounded it, according to the king's own statement, had been built in fifteen days ; within were the famous hanging gardens, raised on lofty arcades, and watered by means of a screw. In the suburb of Borsippa, on the western side of the Euphrates, stood another temple, the modern Birs-i-Nimrud. This was dedicated to Nebo, and had been begun by an earlier king. But it was completed by Nebuchadrezzar, who called it "the temple of the seven lights of the earth," and built it in seven stages, each coloured according to the supposed colours of the seven planets. The upper stages were artificially vitrified, wood having been piled up against the surfaces of the bricks of which they were composed, and then set on fire. Both Borsippa and Babylon were surrounded by a single line of fortification, consisting of a double wall. It was pierced by a hundred gates, all of bronze. So broad were the walls, that two chariots could pass one another upon them. Walls were also built on either side of the river, which flowed through the centre of the city, and was furnished with handsome quays. There were gates in these walls at the end of each of the wide and straight streets by which the city was intersected, and between every gate a ferry-boat plied. Besides the ferry-boats there was also a drawbridge, which was drawn up every night. Such was "great Babylon," which Nebuchadrezzar boasted he had built "for the house of the kingdom, by the might of his power, and for the honour of his majesty."

Records of Nebuchadrezzar's building operations exist in plenty, but of his annals only a small fragment has as yet been discovered. This, however, contains an allusion to his campaign in Egypt, of which Jeremiah and Ezekiel prophesied, and which an over-hasty criticism has denied. The campaign, we learn, took place in the thirty-seventh year of his reign. Other references to it have been detected on the Egyptian monuments, and we gather from these that the Babylonian army swept the whole of the northern part of

Egypt, and penetrated as far south as Assouan, from whence they were forced to retreat by the Egyptian general Hor. Amasis was at this time king of Egypt, having dethroned and murdered Apries, the Pharaoh Hophra of the Bible, whose miserable end had been foretold by Jeremiah (xliv. 30).

No account has yet been discovered among the cuneiform documents of the campaigns of Nebuchadrezzar against Tyre and Judah. But a curious memorial of them was found two years ago on the northern bank of the Nahr el-Kelb, or Dog River, about eight miles to the north of Beyrût. The ancient high road from Damascus to the sea-coast led along the gorge through which this river makes its way to the sea, and traces of it can still be seen cut here and there in the rock. The foreign conquerors of Asia, whether Egyptian or Assyrian have left monuments of themselves carved by the side of this old road, where it winds round a promontory that forms the southern bank of the river. Ramses II, Sennacherib, Esar-haddon, all have recorded their names and deeds upon the face of the cliff; and the obliterated monuments of other and perhaps older kings may still be seen near to them. The existence of these monuments has long been known. But it was never suspected that a long inscription of Nebuchadrezzar also existed on the loftier cliff on the northern side of the river, completely concealed from view under a mass of luxuriant shrubs and drooping maiden-hair fern. It was brought to light by an accident, and though much injured by time and weather is still partly decipherable. Unfortunately, the royal author gives no history in it of his Syrian and Jewish campaigns; the clearest part of the text is occupied only with a list of the wines of the Lebanon, among which the wine of Helbon, near Damascus, was the most highly prized.[1]

Nebuchadrezzar had a long reign of nearly forty-three years. His son and successor, Evil-Merodach ("the man of the god Merodach"), lived hardly three years after his accession, and then was murdered by his brother-in-law, Nergal-sharezer, who seized the crown. The latter calls himself the son of "Bel-suma-iskun, king of Babylon"—a title to which his father could have had no right—and he seems to have been the Rab-Mag (a word of unknown signification) who is mentioned by Jeremiah xxxix. 3) as among the princes of Babylon at the time of the capture of Jerusalem. The chief event of his short reign of four years and four months was the construction of a new palace. His son, who succeeded him, was but a mere boy, and was murdered after a brief reign of four months. The throne was then usurped by Nabu-nahid, the Nabonidos of the Greeks, who does not seem to have belonged to the royal family, and calls his father, "Nabu-balatsu-ikbi, the *Rubu-emga*," which may possibly be the Rab-Mag of the Old Testament. Nabonidos reigned for seventeen years, and witnessed the rise of a new power in the east. This was the empire of Cyrus, about whom the cuneiform records have recently given us information of a most startling kind.

Among the clay documents lately discovered in Babylonia by Mr. Rassam are three inscriptions, which have been published and translated by Sir Henry Rawlinson and Mr. Pinches. The first of these is a cylinder, inscribed by order of Cyrus, the second a tablet which describes the conquest of Babylonia by Cyrus and the

[1] Compare Ezek. xxvii. 18.

causes which led up to it, while the third is an account
given by Nabonidos of his restoration of the temple of
the Moon-god at Haran, and of the temples of the
Sun-god and of Anunit at Sepharvaim.   Haran, we are
told in the last-mentioned record, had been taken and
destroyed by the *Manda*, or " barbarians," of Ekbatana,
and the temple of the Moon-god had shared in the
general ruin of the city. " Then," says Nabonidos, " at the
beginning of my long reign, Merodach, the great lord, and
Sin (the Moon-god), the illuminator of heaven and earth,
the strong one of the universe, revealed unto me a dream.
Merodach spake with me (thus) : ' O Nabonidos, king of
Babylon, go up with the horse of thy chariot ; make
bricks for the Temple of Rejoicing, and let the seat of
Sin, the great lord, enter within it.'   Reverently I spake
to Merodach, the lords of the gods : ' I will build this
house whereof thou hast spoken.   The barbarians went
about it, and their forces were terrible.'   Merodach
answered me : ' The barbarians of whom thou hast
spoken shall not exist, neither they nor their lands, nor
the kings their allies.'   In the third year when it came,
when they (*i.e.*, the barbarians) had caused Cyrus, the
king of Elam, his young servant, to march amongst his
army, they provoked him (to battle) ; the wide-spread
barbarians he overthrew ; he captured Astyages, king of
the barbarians, and seized his treasures ; to his own
land he took (them)."   After this Nabonidos carried
out the will of the gods.   His " vast army " was summoned from Gaza on the one side to the Persian Gulf
on the other, and set to work to restore the temple of
Haran, which had been built three centuries before by
the Assyrian king, Shalmaneser II, and subsequently
repaired by Assur-bani-pal.

Two statements will be noticed in the inscription which will appear strange to students of ancient history. Cyrus is called "the young servant" of Merodach, the patron-deity of Babylon, and "king of Anzan," or Elam, not of Persia. But both statements will be found to be borne out by the two inscriptions of Cyrus himself, which we shall now quote. Both on his cylinder and in the annalistic tablet Cyrus, hitherto supposed to be a Persian and a Zoroastrian monotheist, appears as an Elamite and as a polytheist.

The annalistic tablet, which is unfortunately somewhat mutilated, begins with the first year of the reign of Nabonidos. The first three years after his accession seem to have been occupied with disturbances in Syria. Then, in the sixth year, we are informed, "Astyages gathered (his army) and marched against Cyrus, king of Elam. But the soldiers of Astyages revolted from him, and seized him and delivered him up to Cyrus. Cyrus (proceeded) to the land of Ekbatana, the royal city. The silver, the gold, the furniture, and the spoil of the land of Ekbatana he carried away, and brought the furniture and the spoil which he has taken to the land of Elam.—The seventh year the king (Nabonidos) was in the town of Tema (a suburb of Babylon). The king's son, the nobles, and his soldiers were in Accad (or Northern Babylonia). The king did not go to Babylon, neither did Nebo nor Bel. But they kept a festival; they sacrificed peace-offerings in the temples of Saggil and Zida to the gods for (the preservation) of Babylon and Borsippa. The governor inspected the garden and the temple.—In the eighth year (no event took place).—The ninth year Nabonidos, the king, was in Tema, the king's son, the nobles, and his soldiers

were in Accad. Until the month of Nisan (March) the
king did not go to Babylon, neither did Nebo nor Bel.
But they kept a festival; they sacrificed peace-
offerings to the gods in the temples of Saggil and Zida
for the preservation of Babylon and Borsippa. On the
fifth day of Nisan, the king's mother, who was in the
fortress of the camp on the river Euphrates, above
Sippara, died. The king's son and his soldiers mourned
for her three days running. In the month Sivan (May),
there was a mourning for the king's mother throughout
the land of Accad. In the month Nisan, Cyrus, king of
Persia, collected his soldiers and crossed the Tigris
below Arbela, and the following month (marched)
against the land of . . . . Its king took (his)
silver and himself; he made his own children mount
(the pyre); afterwards both king and children were
(burnt) in the midst (of it)—The tenth year the king
was in Tema; the king's son, the officers, and his
soldiers were in Accad. Until (Nisan) the king (did
not go to Babylon), neither did Nebo nor Bel. But
they kept the festival; they sacrificed peace-offerings to
the gods in the temples (of Saggil and Zida) for the
preservation of Babylon and Borsippa. On the 21st
day of Sivan (the soldiers) of Elam marched into
Accad. A prefect (was appointed?) in Erech.—The
eleventh year the king was in Tema; the king's son,
the nobles, and his soldiers were in Accad. Until Elul
(August), the king did not come forth (to worship) Bel,
but they kept the festival; they sacrificed peace-
offerings (to the gods in the temples of Saggil and
Zida for the preservation of) Babylon and Borsippa."

Here a break occurs in the record. When the inscription becomes legible again we find ourselves transported

to the seventeenth year of Nabonidos, when the tribes on
" the lower sea" or Persian Gulf were in revolt. Cyrus,
who had failed to break through the Babylonian army in
Accad, had spent his time in intriguing with a disaffected
party—probably the Jews—within Babylonia itself, and
at last, when all was ripe, prepared to attack his enemy
from the south-east. Nabonidos now turned to the
gods for help, and had the images of them brought to
Babylon from their various shrines, in the vain hope that
their presence would save the city from capture. " The
gods of Marad, Zamama and the gods of Kis, Beltis
and the gods of Kharsak-kalama, were brought to
Babylon ; up to the end of Elul, the gods of Accad
which are above and below the sky were brought to
Babylon but the gods of Borsippa, of Cuthah, and of
Sippara, were not brought. In the month Tammuz
(June) Cyrus gave battle to the army of Accad in the
town of Rutum, upon the river Nizallat. The men of
Accad broke into revolt. On the 14th day (of the
month) the garrison of Sippara was taken without
fighting. Nabonidos flies. On the 16th day Gobryas,
the governor of Gutium (Kurdistan) and the army of
Cyrus entered Babylon without fighting. Afterwards
he takes Nabonidos, and puts him into fetters in
Babylon. Up to the end of the month Tammuz, some
rebels from Kurdistan kept the gates of the temple of
Saggil closed, but there was nothing in the way of
weapons in the temple of Saggil, nor was there
an opportunity (for fighting). On the 3rd day of
Marchesvan (October), Cyrus entered Babylon. The
roads (?) before him were covered. He grants peace to
the city, to the whole of Babylon Cyrus proclaims
peace. Gobryas, his governor, was appointed over the

(other) governors in Babylon, and from the month Chisleu (November) to the month Adar (February) the gods of Accad, whom Nabonidos had brought to Babylon, were restored to their shrines. On the 11th day of the previous Marchesvan, Gobryas (was appointed) over (Babylon), and the king (Nabonidos) died. From the 27th of Adar to the 3rd of Nisan, (there was) a mourning in Accad; all the people smote their heads. On the 4th day, Kambyses, the son of Cyrus, arranged the burial in the temple of the Sceptre of the World. The priests of the temple of the Sceptre of Nebo went (to it)." The rest of the text, which is very imperfect from this point, describes the honours paid by Cyrus and his son to the Babylonian gods, their sacrifices of victims to Bel, and their restoration of Nebo to his old shrine.

It is at this place that the cylinder of Cyrus comes in to complete the story. Cyrus here says that Nabonidos had neglected the worship of the gods, who accordingly were angry with him: "The gods dwelling within them left their shrines in anger when (Nabonidos) brought them into Babylon. Merodach went about to all men, wherever were their seats; and the men of Sumer and Accad, whom he had sworn should attend him (besought him to return). The favour he granted, he came back; all lands, even the whole of them, rejoiced and ate. And he appointed a king to guide aright in the heart what his hand upholds; Cyrus, king of Elam, he proclaimed by name for the sovereignty: all men everywhere commemorate his name. The men of Kurdistan and all the barbarians (of Ekbatana) he made bow down to his feet, the men of the black-headed race (the Accadians), whom he had conquered with his hand, he governed in justice and righteousness. Merodach, the great lord, the restorer of his people, beheld with joy the deeds of his vicegerent, who was righteous in hand and heart. To his city of Babylon he summoned his march, and he bade him take the road to Babylon; like a friend and a comrade he went at his side. The weapons of his vast army, whose number, like the waters of a river, could not be known, he marshalled at his side. Without fighting or battle he caused him to enter into Babylon; his city of Babylon feared; in a place difficult of access Nabonidos, the king, who worshipped him not, he gave into his hand. The men of Babylon, all of them, (and) the whole of Sumer and Accad, the nobles and priests who had revolted, kissed his feet, they rejoiced in his sovereignty, their faces shone. The god who in his ministry raises the dead to life, who benefits all men in difficulty and prayer, has in goodness drawn nigh to him, has made strong his name. I am Cyrus, the king of legions, the great king, the powerful king, the king of Babylon, the king of Sumer and Accad, the king of the four zones, the son of Kambyses the great king, the king of Elam; the grandson of Cyrus the great king, the king of Elam; the great-grandson of Teispes, the great king, the king of Elam; of the ancient seed-royal, whose rule has been beloved by Bel and Nebo, whose sovereignty they cherished according to the goodness of their hearts. At that time I entered Babylon in peace. With joy and gladness in the palace of the kings I enlarged the seat of my dominion. Merodach, the great lord, (cheered) the heart of his servant, whom the sons of Babylon (obeyed each) year and day. . . . My vast armies he marshalled peacefully in the midst of Babylon; throughout

Sumer and Accad I had no revilers. The sanctuaries
of Babylon and all its fortresses I established in peace.
As for the sons of Babylon . . . . their ruins I
repaired, and I delivered their prisoners. For the work
(of restoring the shrine) of Merodach, the great lord, I
prepared, and he graciously drew nigh unto me, Cyrus,
the king, his worshipper, and to Kambyses, my son, the
offspring of my heart, and to all my army, and in peace
we duly restored its front (in) glory. All the kings who
dwell in the high-places of all regions from the Upper
Sea to the Lower Sea, who dwell in (the high-places) of
the kings of Phœnicia and Sutar, all of them brought
their rich tribute, and in the midst of Babylon kissed
my feet. From (the city of) . . . . to the cities of
Assur and Istar . . . . Accad, Marad, Zamban, Me-
Turnat, and Duran as far as the border of Kurdistan,
the fortresses (which lie) upon the Tigris, wherein from
of old were their seats, I restored the gods who dwelt
within them to their places, and I enlarged (for them)
seats that should be long-enduring ; all their peoples I
assembled, and I restored their lands. And the gods of
Sumer and Accad, whom Nabonidos, to the anger of the
lord of gods (Merodach), had brought into Babylon, I
settled in peace in their sanctuaries by the command of
Merodach, the great lord. In the goodness of their
hearts may all the gods whom I have brought into their
strong places daily intercede before Bel and Nebo that
they should grant me length of days ; may they bless
my projects with prosperity, and may they say to Merodach my lord that Cyrus the king, thy worshipper, and
Kambyses his son (deserve his favour)."

Such are the records, which have risen up, as it were,
out of the tomb, to revolutionise all our previous con-

ceptions of that part of ancient history with which they are concerned. We must give up the belief that Cyrus was a monotheist, bent on destroying the idols of Babylon; on the contrary, from the time when we first hear of him, he is a worshipper of Bel-Merodach, the patron-god of Babylon, and the first care of himself and his son, after his conquest of Babylonia, is to restore the Babylonian gods to the shrines from which they had been impiously removed by Nabonidos. He asks the gods to intercede on his behalf with Bel and Nebo, the two supreme gods of Babylonian worship. It is clear, therefore, that Cyrus was a polytheist, who, like other polytheists in other ages, adopted the gods of the country he had conquered from motives of State policy. The Egyptian monuments give the same account of his son Kambyses. They show that the story told by Herodotus how Kambyses had scoffed at the gods of Egypt, had destroyed their images, and had finally stabbed the sacred bull Apis, was a mere Greek fable. Kambyses appears on contemporaneous monuments as the friend of the Egyptian priests, the adorer of their gods, and the benefactor of their temples. The very bull he was said to have murdered has been discovered in its huge sarcophagus of granite, with a sculpture above, wherein Kambyses is represented as kneeling before the bull-god, while an inscription states that the bull was honoured with the usual funeral, in which Kambyses himself took part.

The theory, accordingly, which held that Cyrus had allowed the Jews to return to their own land, because, like them, he believed in but one supreme god—the Ormazd or good spirit of the Zoroastrian creed—must be abandoned. God consecrated Cyrus to be His instru-

ment in restoring His chosen people to their land, not
because the king of Elam was a monotheist, but
because the period of Jewish trial and punishment had
come to an end.   God's instruments may be unworthy
as well as worthy ; it was through the hardness of heart
of an unbelieving Pharaoh that the deliverance from
Egypt had been accomplished in days long before.   Nor
is there any contradiction between the treatment
actually experienced by the Babylonians and that which
is predicted for them in the Book of Isaiah.   The
language of the prophet is necessarily figurative, and
when he declares (Isa. xlvi. 1, 2) that Bel and Nebo had
gone into captivity, nothing more is meant than that
the people whose gods they were, and whom they
represented, had passed under the yoke of a foreign
conqueror.

And yet, though the prophet's language was thus
figurative, the prediction was eventually fulfilled in a
very literal way.   The empire of Cyrus was broken up
after the death of Kambyses, and had to be reconquered
by Darius the son of Hystaspes, the real founder of the
Persian Empire.   Darius was a Zoroastrian monotheist
as well as a Persian, and under him and his successors
polytheism ceased to be the religion of the State.
Twice during his reign he had to besiege Babylon.
Hardly had he been proclaimed king when it revolted
under a certain Nidinta-Bel, who called himsel, "Nebuchadrezzar, the son of Nabonidos.   A cameo exists
with his helmeted profile, engraved by a Greek artist,
and surrounded by the words, "To Merodach, his lord,
Nebuchadrezzar, the king of Babylon, has made (it)
for his life;" unless, perhaps, Professor Schrader is right
in referring the portrait, not to the pretender, but to

the real Nebuchadrezzar of Biblical history. Babylon endured a siege of two years, and was at last captured by Darius only by the help of a stratagem. Six years afterwards it again rose in revolt, under an Armenian, who professed, like his predecessor, to be " Nebuchadrezzar, the son of Nabonidos." Once more, however, it was besieged and taken, and this time the pretender was put to death by impalement. His predecessor, Nidinta-Bel, seems to have been slain while the Persian troops were forcing their way into the captured city. After the second capture of Babylon Darius pulled down its walls; and his son Xerxes completed the work of destruction by destroying the great temple of Bel, and carrying away the golden image of the god.

In Nidinta-Bel the line of independent Babylonian kings may be regarded as having come to an end, since the leader of the second revolt was not a native, but an Armenian settler. To him, therefore, we may apply the magnificent description of the death of the last Babylonian monarch on the battle-field, and his descent into the under-world, which we read in Isaiah xiv. Illustrations have been taken by the prophet from Babylonian mythology, in order to heighten the horror of the scene. The king of Babylonia is compared to the morning star, whose movements the Babylonians had been the first of mankind to record. He is represented as saying in his heart, " I will ascend into heaven, I will exalt my throne above the (other) stars of God : I will sit also upon the mount of the assembly (of the gods) in the furthest regions of the north." This mount, as we have seen in an earlier chapter, was the Olympos of the Accadians, by whom it was called Kharsak-kurra "the mountain of the east." Its peak was the pivot on which the sky rested, and it was therefore also known as "the mountain of the world." It lay far away in the regions of the north-east, the entrance, as it was supposed, to the lower world, and it was sometimes identified with the mountain of Nizir, the modern Rowandiz, on whose summit the ark of the Chaldean Noah was believed to have rested. From the heights of this mountain, where he had vainly dreamed of sitting among the gods, the Babylonian king was to be hurled into the world below. Here again the prophet borrows his illustration from the mythology of Accad. The heroes of the past are placed before us seated in Hades on their shadowy thrones, from which they rise to greet the arrival of their new comrade.

The best commentary on the description is to be found in the words of an old Babylonian poem, which tells of the descent of the goddess Istar into Hades, in search of her dead husband Tammuz. The poem opens as follows :—

"To Hades, the land whence none return, the land of darkness,
  Istar the daughter of the Moon-god inclined her ear,
  Yea, the daughter of the Moon-god inclined her ear.
  To the house of darkness, the dwelling of the god Irkalla,
  To the house out of which there is no exit,
  To the road from which there is no return,
  To the house from whose entrance the light is taken,
  The place where dust is their nourishment, and mud their food ;
  Light is never seen, in darkness they dwell."

Parallel with this is the description of Hades, supposed to be given by the dead friend of Gisdhubar, in the great Chaldean epic in which the account of the deluge is embodied. Here we read—

"To Hades, the land whence none return, I turn myself,
I spread like a bird my hands.
I descend, I descend, to the house of darkness, the dwelling of the god Irkalla.
To the house out of which there is no exit.
To the road from which there is no return,
To the house from whose entrance the light is taken,
The place where dust is their nourishment, and mud their food,
And its chiefs are like birds covered with feathers;
Light is never seen, in darkness they dwell.
In that house, O my friend, which I shall enter.
There is treasured up for me a crown.
With those wearing crowns, who from days of old ruled the the earth.
To whom the gods Anu and Bel have given names of rule."

But it is time for us to return to the inscriptions of Cyrus. Next to the fact that he was a polytheist, the most startling revelation they make is that he was not a king of Persia at all. Persia seems to have been acquired by him after his conquest of Astyages, at some time between the sixth and ninth year of Nabonidos. Both he and his ancestors were kings of Anzan or Elam. It is true, he could trace his descent back to a member of the royal Persian clan, Teispes, who appears to have taken possession of Elam during the troublous period that followed the fall of Assyria, and to have resigned his Persian dominions to his son Ariaramnes, the great-grandfather of Darius. It must be this conquest of Elam which was prophesied by Jeremiah at the

beginning of Zedekiah's reign (Jer. xlix. 34-39), and
the result of it was to make Cyrus an Elamite in education and religion. The empire which he founded was
not a Persian one; Darius, the son of Hystaspes, was
the real founder of that. It was only as the predecessor
of Darius, and for the sake of intelligibility to the readers
of a later day, that Cyrus could be called a king of
Persia, as he is in the Book of Ezra, where the original
words of his proclamation, "king of Elam" have been
changed into the more familiar and intelligible "king of
Persia" (Ez. i. 2.) Elsewhere in the Bible (Isa. xxi.
1-10), where the invasion of Babylonia is described,
there is no mention of Persia, only of Elam and Media,
that is to say, of the ancestral dominions of Cyrus and
that kingdom of Ekbatana which he had annexed.
This is in strict accordance with the revelations of the
monuments, and is a most interesting testimony to
the accuracy of the Old Testament records.

Another fact of an equally revolutionary kind which
the inscriptions teach us is that Babylon was not
besieged and taken by Cyrus. It opened his gates to his
general long before he came near it, and needed neither
fighting nor battle for its occupation. It thus becomes
evident that the siege of Babylon described by Herodotus really belongs to the reign of Darius, and has
been transferred by tradition to the reign of Cyrus, and
that the late Mr. Bosanquet was right in asserting that
the Darius of the Book of Daniel is Darius the son of
Hystaspes. Belshazzar, as we know from an inscription of Nabonidos, which mentions him, was the eldest
son of that monarch, and he is no doubt the "king's
son" who commanded the Babylonian army, according
to the tablet translated above.

But besides the main facts to be derived from these newly found inscriptions, there is much else in them which is worthy of regard.   This is especially the case with the inscription on the clay cylinder, in which we find a reference to the restoration of the Babylonian captives to their several homes.   The experience of Cyrus had taught him that the old Assyrian and Babylonian system of transporting conquered nations was an error, and did but introduce a dangerously disaffected people into the country to which they had been brought. Through this conviction, which seemed to Cyrus himself merely the result of his own experience and political sagacity, God worked to bring about the fulfilment of His promises to the Jewish exiles.   Those who chose to return to Jerusalem were allowed to do so, and there rebuild a fortress which Cyrus considered would be useful to him as a check upon Egypt.   The nations which had been brought from east and west were restored to their lands, along with their gods, whom they were henceforth to worship in peace.   Among them, as we learn from the Old Testament, were the captives of Judah, the worshippers of the one true God.

Another fact which we gather from the words of Cyrus is that Nabonidos had offended the Babylonian priest-hood, and had been accused by some of them of impiety. His removal of the images of the local deities from their shrines seems to have been regarded as a peculiar sin ; and Cyrus goes so far as to assert that Nabonidos had brought them into Babylon, "to the anger of the lord of gods." Indeed, he even says that the Baby-lonian king had not worshipped the patron god of his own capital.   How little, however, this statement was really justified may be seen from the inscription of

Nabonidos quoted above, in which reference is made for the first time to Cyrus, "the young servant" of Merodach.

The language used of himself by Cyrus reminds us sometimes of the inspired words in which he is spoken of in the prophecies of Isaiah. When he says that he "governed in justice and righteousness," and that Merodach "beheld with joy the deeds of his vicegerent, who was righteous in hand and heart," we cannot help thinking of God's declaration that He had "raised him up in righteousness," (Isa. xlv. 13). When he says that "Merodach, who in his ministry raises the dead to life, who benefits all men in difficulty and prayer, has in goodness drawn nigh to him, has made strong his name," we almost fancy we hear an echo of the words of Scripture: "For Jacob My servant's sake, and Israel Mine elect, I have even called thee by thy name; I have surnamed thee, though thou hast not known Me. I am the LORD, and there is none else, there is no God beside Me. I girded thee, though thou hast not known Me " (Isa. xlv. 4, 5).

The title given to Merodach—"the god who raises the dead to life "—is a remarkable one, but it was a title which was applied to the god as early as the Accadian epoch. In the religious hymns of the Accadians, Merodach plays the part of a mediator and intercessor; if the gods are angry, it is Merodach who intercedes for man. Mankind, in fact, are his especial care; he was supposed to heal their diseases and to raise them after death to life. Whether there was any reference here to the doctrine of the resurrection is doubtful: more probably nothing further was meant than that the spirit of the dead man, through the help of Merodach, was

allowed to drink of " the waters of life," that bubbled up
in Hades beneath the golden throne of the spirits of
earth, and so to ascend to the Accadian heaven, "the
land of the silver sky," where the heroes lay reclined
among the gods on couches, feasting at banquets which
knew no end.

Merodach was originally the Sun-god, and when
Babylonia passed into the hands of the Semites he
still continued to be worshipped, as the interceding god
who hears prayers and " raises the dead to life." But he
was now more specially honoured as Bel or Baal, "lord"
a title which properly belonged to an older deity, but
which came in time to be almost confined to Merodach,
alone. When Bel and Nebo are mentioned together in
the Bible (Isa. xlvi. 1), it is Merodach, the tutelary
divinity of Babylon, that is meant, Nebo, "the prophet,"
to whom peculiar honour was paid at Babylon after the
rise of the dynasty of Nebuchadrezzar, being usually
associated with him.

A large number of prayers have been discovered
addressed for the most part to Merodach, though there
are some which are addressed also to the other deities.
These prayers are written in Assyrian, and constitute a
sort of manual of devotion. They are seldom of great
length, one of the longest being a prayer after a bad
dream, which is, however, addressed to the goddess
Istar as well as to Merodach. Portions of it have been
lost ; what remains may be quoted as an example of
this species of literature, and is as follows : " May the
lord set my prayer at rest, (may he remove) my heavy
(sin) ! May the lord (grant) a return of favour. By
day direct unto death all that disquiets me. O my
goddess, be gracious unto me ; when (wilt thou hear)

my prayer? May they pardon my sin, my wickedness, (and) my transgression. May the exalted one deliver, may the holy one love. May the seven winds carry away my groaning. May the worm lay it low, may the bird bear it upwards to heaven. May a shoal of fish carry it away; may the river bear it along. May the creeping thing of the field come unto me; may the waters of the river as they flow cleanse me. Enlighten me like a mask of gold. Food and drink perpetually before thee may I get. Heap up the worm, take away his life. The steps of thine altar, thy many ones, may I ascend. With the worm make me pass, and may I be kept with thee. Make me to be fed, and may a favourable dream come. May the dream I dream be favourable; may the dream I dream be fulfilled, May the dream I dream turn to prosperity. May Makhir, the god of dreams, settle upon my head. Let me enter Beth-Saggil, the palace of the gods, the temple of the lord. Give me unto Merodach, the merciful, to prosperity, even to prospering hands. May thy entering be exalted, may thy divinity be glorious; may the men of my city extol thy mighty deeds."

The tone of this prayer is not very high, and it reveals how much superstition was mixed with even the best aspirations of Assyrian spiritual life. It is, therefore, somewhat surprising that a series of penitential psalms exists, coming down from the earliest period of Babylonian history, which breathe a much more exalted and purer spirit. These psalms are not written in Accadian, but in the closely-allied dialect of Sumer or Shinar, and an Assyrian interlinear translation is attached to them. From time to time expressions that occur in them remind us of the Book of Psalms. No more suitable way can be found of concluding our review of the illustrations of the Old Testament Scriptures afforded by modern discovery, than by giving at full length a translation of one of these touching relics of old time. In reading it we do indeed feel that even in the darkest ages of ignorance and heathenism God was still moving the hearts of men, "that they should seek the Lord, if haply they might feel after Him and find Him :"

"My Lord is wroth in his heart ; may he be appeased again.
May God be appeased again, for I knew not that I sinned.
May Istar, my mother, be appeased again, for I knew not that I sinned.
God knoweth that I knew not ; may he be appeased.
Istar, my mother, knoweth that I knew not ; may she be appeased.
May the heart of my God be appeased.
May the heart of Istar, my mother, be appeased.
May God and Istar, my mother, be appeased.
May God cease from his anger.
May Istar, my mother, (cease from her anger).
The transgression (I committed my God) knew.
            [The next few lines are obliterated.]
The transgression (I committed Istar, my mother, knew).
(My tears) I drink like the waters of the sea.
That which was forbidden by my God, I ate without knowing.
That which was forbidden by Istar, my mother, I trampled on without knowing.
O my Lord, my transgression is great, many are my sins.
O my God, my transgression is great, many are my sins.
O Istar, my mother, my transgression is great, many are my sins.
O my God, who knowest that I knew not, my transgression is great, many are my sins.

O Istar, my mother, who knowest that I knew not, my transgression is great, many are my sins.

The transgression that I committed I knew not.

The sin that I sinned I knew not.

The forbidden thing did I eat.

The forbidden thing did I trample on.

My Lord, in the anger of his heart, has punished me.

God in the strength of his heart has received me.

Istar, my mother, has seized upon me and put me to grief.

God, who knoweth that I knew not, has afflicted me.

Istar, my mother, who knoweth that I knew not, has caused darkness.

I prayed and none takes my hand.

I wept and none held my palm.

I cry aloud ; but there is none that will hear me.

I am in darkness and hiding, I dare not look up.

To God I refer my distress, I utter my prayer.

The feet of Istar, my mother, I embrace.

To God, who knoweth that I knew not, my prayer I utter.

To Istar, my mother, who knoweth that I knew not, my prayer I address.

[The next four lines are lost.]

How long, O God (shall I suffer)?

How long, O Istar, my mother (shall I suffer)?

How long, O God, who knoweth that I knew not, (shall I feel thy) strength ?

How long, O Istar, my mother, who knoweth that I knew not, shall thy heart (be angry)?

Thou writest the number (?) of mankind, and none knoweth it.

Thou callest man by his name, and what does he know ?

Whether he shall be afflicted, or whether he shall be prosperous, there is no man that knows.

O my God, thou givest not rest to thy servant.

In the waters of the raging flood take his hand.

The sin he has sinned turn into good.

Let the wind carry away the transgression I have committed.

Destroy my manifold wickedness like a garment.

O my God, seven times seven are my transgressions, my transgressions are (ever) before me.[1]

[1] The following chronological table will assist the reader in understanding the sequence of events in the preceding chapter :—

B.C.

609. Battle of Megiddo ; Josiah slain ; Pharaoh Necho overruns Western Asia.

606. Necho defeated at Carchemish by Nebuchadrezzar ; foundation of the Babylonian empire.

604. Nebuchadrezzar succeeds his father Nabopolassar.

599. Jerusalem captured ; Jehoiachin sent to Babylon.

588. Destruction of Jerusalem ; murder of Gedaliah.

567. The Babylonians overrun Egypt, then governed by Amasis.

561. Nebuchadrezzar succeeded by his son Evil-Merodach.

559. Nergal-sharezer, son of Bel-sum-iskun, seizes the Babylonian crown.

555. Nergal-sharezer succeeded by Laborosoarchod.

555. The crown seized by Nabonidos, son of Nabu-balatsu-ikbi.

552. The dream of Nabonidos.

549. Conquest of Astyages of Ekbatana (Media) by Cyrus, king of Elam.

548. Death of "the king's mother" (Nitokris).

538. Overthrow and death of Nabonidos ; Cyrus occupies Babylon.

529. Death of Cyrus and accession of Kambyses.

521. Darius, the son of Hystaspes, elected to the throne of Persia.

520–19. Revolt of Babylon under Nidinta-Bel.

513. Second revolt of Babylon under Arakha.

APPENDIX I.

The text of the Treaty between the Hittites and Ramses II (Dr. Brugsch's translation) :—

In the year 21, in the month of Tybi, on the 21st day of the month, in the reign of king Ramessu Mi-Amun, the dispenser of life eternally and for ever, the worshipper of the divinities, Amun-Ra (of Thebes), Hor-em-khu (of Heliopolis), Ptah (of Memphis), Mut, the lady of the Asher Lake (near Karnak), and Khonsu, the peace-loving, there took place a public sitting on the throne of Horus among the living, resembling his father, Hor-em-khu in eternity, in eternity, evermore.

On that day the king was in the city of Ramses (Zoan), presenting his peace-offerings to his father, Amun-ra, and to the gods, Hor-em-khu-Tum, the lord of Heliopolis (On), and to Amun of Ramessu Mi-Amun, to Ptah of Ramessu Mi-Amun, and to Sutekh, the strong, the son of Nut, the goddess of heaven, that they might grant to him many thirty years' jubilee feasts, and innumerable happy years, and the subjection of all peoples under his feet for ever.

Then came forward the ambassador of the king and the governor (of his house, by name . . . . , and presented the ambassadors) of the great king of the Hittites (Khita), Khita-sir, who were sent to Pharaoh to propose friendship with the king, Ramessu Mi-Amun, the dispenser of life eternally and for ever, just as his father, the Sun-god (dispenses it), each day.

This is the copy of the contents of the silver tablet, which the great king of the Hittites, Khita-sir, had caused to be made, and which was presented to the Pharaoh by the hand of his ambassador Tartibus and his ambassador Ra-mes, to propose friendship to the king, Ramessu Mi-Amun, the bull among the princes, who places his boundary-marks where it pleases him in all lands.

The treaty which had been proposed by the great king of the Hittites, Khita-sir, the powerful, the son of Maro-sir, the great king of the Hittites, the powerful, the grandson of Sapalili, the great king of the Hittites, the powerful, on the silver tablet, to Ramessu Mi-Amun, the great prince of Egypt, the powerful, the grandson of Ramessu I, the great king of Egypt, the powerful,—this was a good treaty for friendship and concord, which assured peace (and established concord) for a longer period than was previously the case for a long time. For it was the agreement of the great prince of Egypt in common with the great king of the Hittites, that the god should not allow enmity to exist between them, on the basis of a treaty.

To wit, in the times of Mauthaner, the great king of the Hittites, my brother, he was at war with (Meneptah Seti I) the great prince of Egypt.

But now, from this very day forward, Khita-sir, the great king of the Hittites, shall look upon this treaty, so that the agreement may remain, which the Sun-god, Ra, has made, which the god Sutekh has made, for the people of Egypt and for the people of the Hittites, that there should be no enmity between them for evermore.

And these are the contents :—

Khita-sir, the great king of the Hittites, is in covenant with Ramessu Mi-Amun, the great prince of Egypt, from this very day forward, that there may subsist a good friendship and a good understanding between them for evermore.

He shall be my ally; he shall be my friend. I will be his ally; I will be his friend; for ever.

To wit: in the time of Mauthaner, the great king of the Hittites, his brother, Khita-sir, after his murder, placed himself on the throne of his father as the great king of the Hittites. I strove for friendship with Ramessu Mi-Amun, the great prince of Egypt, and it is (my wish) that the friendship and the concord may be better than the friendship and the concord which before existed, and which was broken.

I declare: I, the great king of the Hittites, will hold together with (Ramessu Mi-Amun) the great prince of Egypt, in good friendship and good concord. The sons of the sons of the great king of the Hittites will hold together and be friends with the sons of the sons of Ramessu Mi-Amun, the great prince of Egypt.

In virtue of our treaty for concord, and in virtue of our agreement (for friendship, let the people) of Egypt (be bound in friendship) with the people of the Hittites. Let a like friendship and a like concord subsist in such measure for ever.

Never let enmity rise between them. Never let the great king of the Hittites invade the land of Egypt, it anything has been plundered from it (the land of the Hittites). Never let Ramessu Mi-Amun, the great prince of Egypt, overstep the boundary of the land (of the Hittites, if anything shall have been plundered) from it (the land of Egypt).

The just treaty which existed in the times of Sapalili, the great king of the Hittites, likewise the just treaty which existed in the times of Mauthaner, the great king of the Hittites, my brother, that will I keep.

Ramessu Mi-Amun, the great prince of Egypt, declares that he will keep it. (We have come to an understanding about it) with one another at the same time from this day forward, and we will fulfil it, and will act in a righteous manner.

If another shall come as an enemy to the lands of Ramessu Mi-Amun, the great prince of Egypt, then let him send an embassy to the great king of the Hittites to this effect : " Come, and make me stronger than him." Then shall the great king of the Hittites (assemble his warriors), and the king of the Hittites (shall come) and smite his enemies. But if it should not be the wish of the great king of the Hittites to march out in person, then he shall send his warriors and his chariots that they may smite his enemies. Otherwise (he would incur) the wrath of Ramessu Mi-Amun (the great prince of Egypt. And if Ramessu Mi-Amun, the great prince of Egypt, should banish for a crime) subjects from his country, and they should commit further crime against him, then shall the king of the Hittites come forward to kill them. The great king of the Hittites shall act in common with (the great prince of Egypt).

(If another should come as an enemy to the lands of the great king of the Hittites, then shall he send an embassy to the great prince of Egypt with the request that) he would come in great power to kill his enemies ; and if it be the intention of Ramessu Mi-Amun, the great prince of Egypt, (himself) to come, he shall (smite the enemies of the great king of the Hittites. If it is not the intention of the great prince of Egypt to march out in person, then he shall send his warriors and his two)-horse chariots, while he sends back the answer to the people of the Hittites.

If any subjects of the great king of the Hittites have offended him, then Ramessu Mi-Amun (the great prince of Egypt, shall not receive them in his land, but shall advance to kill them) . . . . the oath with the wish to say, I will go . . . . until . . . . Ramessu Mi-Amun, the great prince of Egypt, living for ever . . . . that he may be given for them (?) to the lord, and that Ramessu Mi-Amun, the great prince of Egypt, may speak according to his agreement for evermore . . . .

(If servants shall flee away) out of the territories of Ramessu Mi-Amun, the great prince of Egypt, to betake themselves to) the great king of the Hittites, the great king of the Hittites shall not receive them, but the great king of the Hittites shall give them up to Ramessu Mi-Amun, the great prince of Egypt (that they may be punished).

If servants of Ramessu Mi-Amun, the great prince of Egypt, leave his country, and betake themselves to the land of the Hittites, to make themselves servants of another, they shall not remain in the land of the Hittites, (but shall be given up) to Ramessu Mi-Amun, the great prince of Egypt.

If, on the other hand, there should flee away (servants of the great king of the Hittites, in order to betake themselves to) Ramessu Mi-Amun, the great prince of Egypt, (in order to stay in Egypt), then those who have come from the land of the Hittites in order to betake themselves to Ramessu Mi-Amun, the great prince of Egypt, shall not be (received) by Ramessu Mi-Amun, the great prince of Egypt, (but) the great prince of Egypt, Ramessu Mi-Amun, (shall deliver them up to the great king of the Hittites.

And if shall leave the land of the Hittites persons) of skilled mind, so that they come to the land of Egypt to make themselves servants of another, then Ramessu Mi-Amun shall not allow them to settle, he shall deliver them up to the great king of the Hittites.

When this (treaty) shall be known (by the inhabitants of the land of Egypt and of the land of the Hittites, then shall they not offend against it, for all that stands written on) the silver tablet, these are words which will have been approved by the company of the gods, among the male gods, and among the female gods, among those, namely, of the land of the Hittites, and by the company of the gods among the male gods and among the female gods, among those, namely, of the land of Egypt. They are witnesses for me (to the validity) of these words, (which they have allowed.

This is the catalogue of the gods of the land of the Hittites:—

Sutekh of the city of) Tunep,
Sutekh of the land of the Hittites,
Sutekh of the city of Arnema,
Sutekh of the city Zaranda [or Ta-Orontes],
Sutekh of the city of Pilka [or Pairaka],
Sutekh of the city of Khisasap,
Sutekh of the city of Sarsu,
Sutekh of the city of Aleppo,
Sutekh of the city of .   .   .   . ,
(Sutekh of the city of.   .   .   .),
Sutekh of the city of Sarpina,
Astartha [or Antarata] of the land of the Hittites,
The god of the land of Zaiath-khirri,
The god of the land of Ka . . .,
The god of the land of Kher . . .,
The goddess of the city of Akh . . .,

(The goddess of the city of . . . .) and of the land of A . . . ua,

The goddesss of the land of Zaina,

The god of the land of . . nath . . er.

(I have invoked these male and these) female (gods of the land of the Hittites, these are the gods) of the land, as (witnesses to) my oath. (With them have been associated the male and the female gods) of the mountains, and of the rivers of the land of the Hittites, the gods of the land of Kazawatana. Amun, Ra, Sutekh, and the male and female gods of the land of Egypt, of the earth, of the sea, of the winds, and of the storms.

With regard to the commandment which the silver tablet contains for the people of the Hittites and for the people of Egypt, he who shall not observe it shall be given over (to the vengeance) of the company of the gods of the Hittites, and shall be given over (to the vengeance of the) company of the gods of Egypt, (he) and his house and his servants.

But he who shall observe these commandments, which the silver tablet contains, whether he be of the people of the Hittites or (of the people of the Egyptians), because he has not neglected them, the company of the gods of the land of the Hittites and the company of the gods of the land of Egypt shall secure his reward and preserve life (for him) and his servants, and those who are with him and who are with his servants.

If there flee away of the inhabitants (one from the land of Egypt), or two or three, and they betake themselves to the great king of the Hittites, (the great king of the Hittites shall not) allow them (to remain, but he shall) deliver them up, and send them back to Ramessu Mi-Amun, the great prince of Egypt.

Now with regard to the (inhabitant of the land of Egypt),
who is delivered up to Ramessu Mi-Amun, the great prince of
Egypt, his fault shall not be avenged upon him, his (house)
shall not be taken away, nor his (wife), nor his (children).
There shall not be (put to death his mother, neither shall he be
punished in his eyes, nor in his mouth, nor on the soles of his
feet), so that thus no crime shall be brought forward against
him.

In the same way shall it be done, if inhabitants of the land
of the Hittites take to flight, be it one alone, or two or three,
to betake themselves to Ramessu Mi-Amun, the great prince of
Egypt ; Ramessu Mi-Amun, the great prince of Egypt, shall
cause them to be seized, and they shall be delivered up to the
great king of the Hittites.

(With regard to) him who (is delivered up, his crime shall not
be brought forward against him). His (house) shall not be
taken away, nor his wives nor his children, nor his people ; his
mother shall not be put to death, he shall not be punished in
his eyes, nor on his mouth, nor on the soles of his feet, nor
shall any accusation be brought forward against him.

That which is in the middle of this silver tablet and on its
front side is a likeness of the god Sutekh . . . . surrounded
by an inscription to this effect : "This is the (picture) of the
god Sutekh, the king of heaven and (earth)." At the time
(?) of the treaty which the great king of the Hittites, Khita-sir
made . . . .

APPENDIX II.

LIST OF THE MONTHS OF THE ASSYRIAN YEAR:—

English name.	Assyrian name.	Meaning.	Hebrew name.	Accadian name.	Zodiacal sign.
March	Nisannu	Month of opening	Nisan	Altar of the righteous	Aries
April	Airu	The bright	Iyyar	The directing bull	Taurus
May	Sivanu	Month of brick-making	Sivan	Month of the bricks / Month of the Twins	Gemini
June	Duzu	Month of the Sun-god, Tammuz	Tammuz	Month of sowing	Cancer
July	Abu		Ab	Fire that makes fire	Leo
August	Ululu	Month of the spirit	Elul	Month of the errand of Istar	Virgo
September	Tasritu	Month of the Sanctuary	Tisri	Month of the holy mound (of Babylon)	Libra
October	Arakh-savna	The eighth month	Marchesvan	Month opposite the foundation	Scorpio
November	Kisilivu, or Kuzallu		Chisleu	Month of clouds (?)	Sagittarius
December	Tabitu	The good month	Tebet	The cave of the rising sun	Capricornus
January	Sabatu		Sebat	Month of the curse of rain	Aquarius
February	Addaru	The dark month	Adar	Month of the sowing of seed	Pisces

The Hebrew Ve-Adar corresponded to the Assyrian *arakh-maktru*, or incidental month.

APPENDIX III.

Translation of a cylinder of Nabonidos, king of Babylonia, containing the name of Belshazzar. The cylinder is one of four, each containing the same text and buried. at the four corners of the temple of Sin, the Moon-god, at Mugheir or Ur.

Col. I.

"Nabonidos, the king of Babylon, the beautifier of Bit-Saggil and Bit-Zida, the worshipper of the great gods, am I. The temple of the king who provides plenty (Sin), the tower of the temple of Gis-nu-gal,[1] which is within Ur, which Lig-Bagas, an ancient king, had made but did not finish, Dungi, his son, completed its work. I looked into the cylinders of Lig-Bagas and Dungi his son, and (read) how Lig-Bagas had made this tower but did not finish it, and how Dungi his son completed its work. Subsequently this tower became old, and accordingly above the old platform which Lig-Bagas and Dungi his son had made I built the walls[2] of this tower, as of old, with cement and brick, and I founded and erected them for Sin, the lord of the gods of heaven and earth, the king of the gods, even the gods of gods, who inhabit heaven, the great ones, the lord of the temple of Gis-nu-gal within Ur, my lord."

[1] "The wood of the great prince."
[2] Literally, "I took the framework."

Col. II.

"O Sin, lord of the gods, king of the gods of heaven and
earth, even the gods of gods, who inhabit heaven, the great
ones, for this temple, with joy at thy entrance, may thy lips
establish the blessings of Bit-Saggil, Bit-Zida, and Bit-Gis-nu-
gal, the temples of thy great divinity; set the fear of thy great
divinity in the hearts of his (*i.e.*, Nabonidos') men that they err
not; for thy great divinity may their foundations remain firm
like the heavens.   As for me, Nabonidos, the king of Babylon,
preserve me from sinning against thy great divinity, and grant
me the gift of a life of long days; and plant in the heart of
Bilu-sarra-utsur (Belshazzar), the eldest son, the offspring of my
heart, reverence for thy great divinity, and never may he incline
to sin; with fulness of life may he be satisfied."

INDEX.

Omri, tribute of, 105.

Palestine, early travels in, 59.
Paradise, site of, 26.
Pharaoh, origin of word, 51.
Pharaoh Necho, 136.
Phœnician ritual, 68.
Phut, 41.
Pishon, origin of word, 26.
Pithom, site of, 62.
Pool of Siloam, site of, 84 ; recent discoveries at, 90.

Ramses, sites of, 60.
Rawlinson's studies of inscriptions, 12.
Rimmon, 104.
Rimmon-nirari, conquests of, 107.
Rowandiz, 35.

Sabbath, Babylonian, 24.
Samaria, capture of, 113 ; re-settlement of, 114.
Sarah, origin of word, 46.
Sargon, wars of, 116 ; capture of Jerusalem by, 117 ; death of, 120.
Scythians, the, 131.
Sennacherib, wars of, 120 ; inscription of, 120 ; bas-relief of, 124 ; at
    Lachish, 125 ; defeat of, 126 ; murder of, 127.
Shalmaneser II, campaigns of, 101 ; inscription of, 102 ; conquers Hazael,
    105 ; erects his own image, 105 ; obelisk of, 106.
Shem, 38.
Shishak, capture of Jerusalem by, 100.
Siloam inscription, discovery of, 83 ; site of, 84 ; translation of, 87 ;
    language of, 88 ; date of, 88.
Sisuthros, adventures of, 28 ; translation of legend concerning, 29 ; meaning
    of the name, 36.
Sumirians, the, 20.

Tariff of Sacrifices, translation of, 69.
Tiglath-Pileser, campaigns of, 108 ; death of, 112.
Two Brothers, Tale of the, 54.

Ur, site of, 46.

Harrison & Sons, Printers in Ordinary to Her Majesty, St. Martin's Lane.

www.ingramcontent.com/pod-product-compliance
Lightning Source LLC
Chambersburg PA
CBHW020536270326
41927CB00006B/596